A MIND OF THEIR OWN

A Lawyer's Life:
Six Decades in Celebration of Some of America's Most
Remarkable Entrepreneurs, Artists and Adventurers

TONY CURTO

A MIND OF THEIR OWN

A Lawyer's Life: Six Decades in Celebration of Some of America's Most Remarkable Entrepreneurs, Artists and Adventurers

ISBN 979-8-9872444-0-1 paperback
ISBN 979-8-9872444-7-0 hardcover

Published by Onward Publishing, Inc.
Port Jefferson, NY 11777

Jacket design by Anthony Stiso

First Edition

ADVANCE PRAISE FOR *A MIND OF THEIR OWN*

"Tony Curto's amazing adventure, as told in *A Mind of Their Own*, captures some of the most significant people and events that occurred over of the last sixty years. His unique story-telling style brings each figure to life, in chapter after chapter. Curto's career as New York attorney reminds me of the Harry Chapin lyric, "No straight lines make up my life." Anyone who loves history—or just a good story—has to read this book."

—**Jim Gaughran**, New York State Senator,
5ᵗʰ Senate District

"Tony Curto's *A Mind of Their Own* flows effortlessly, as if he is sitting in your living room, telling the latest story of the fascinating people and events he was dealing with in his law practice. His style transitions easily from international intrigue with the Russian Nobel-Prize winning author Aleksandr Solzhenitsyn, to the ground-breaking battle over free agency with pro football star Freeman MacNeil, to the intense competition of international sailboat championship races—with just a deft touch of the law that helped his clients achieve their goals. You will be captivated with the true-life stories about special people who profoundly affected our world, guided by Curto's counsel. All told, this book is a true American story, one that readers will not want to put down once they start.

—**Bill Jorch Sr.**, Navigator for Ted Turner on
the Americas Cup yacht, *Courageous*

"I was mesmerized by Tony Curto's writing—from his childhood experiences to working for the great *New York Times* correspondent, Harrison Salisbury. His style is so quick, yet full of thoughtful insights. I found myself racing along, nodding at his delightful observations. This book will resonate with every baby boomer wanting to find his or her niche, and with everyone who enjoys a good nonfiction journey—each chapter dedicated to another amazing personality."
—**Melissa Barasch**, Creative Director, Onward Publishing

"Tony Curto's depiction of his early childhood was like a trip back into time, when life was simpler without all the trappings we deal with today. It reminds me that so much of what goes on in our early years really does make us who we are today. It was such a pleasurable read, transporting the reader much like a fictional novel. Curto is a gifted writer."
—**Robert J. Eckhardt**, Founder and managing partner, Eckhardt & Company, P.C.

"There are many parts to Tony Curto's story—small scenes, colorful characters, vivid images. His thoughts move forward, sometimes in a stroll, sometimes at a gallop. But Curto is never someone who just chats. He always speaks with thoughtful, carefully chosen words, circling around a tough question (honesty, fidelity, happiness, ambition, wealth, self-sufficiency, systematic legal injustice, boat design), testing hypotheses, studying the opposition, identifying logical obstacles and looking for workaround solutions. For Tony Curto, a memoir does not simply recount a string of events and characters. It must answer a strategy, and it must achieve a worthy goal."
—**Donald Condit**, Retired President, Condit Marketing Communications

"In *A Mind of Their Own,* Tony Curto delivers 19 compelling stories, from smuggling manuscripts out of the Soviet Union, to confronting a sailboat racing crew that turned out to be smugglers themselves—of marijuana. Tony gives us an intimate look at some iconic figures across the last six decades. Through the eyes of this curious, altruistic dealmaker, we gain insights into some of the events that impacted the fields of entertainment, sports, industry, religion, music— and pornography. Each story can stand on its own; each is compelling and intriguing. The authenticity is apparent. In sharing these stories as legal counsel to many famous entrepreneurs, artists, inventors, and other celebrities, Tony Curto provides the reader with some history and entertainment, while always steering a moral compass to True North."

—**Nick Fitterman, MD** Executive Director of Huntington
Hospital and Professor of Medicine

"Curto writes with admirable lucidity—even potentially forbidding questions about legal technicalities are rendered fully accessible to the layperson. While the author's vivid stories focus on celebrities, it is not their fame per se that sets them apart for Curto—this remembrance is not the expression of infatuation with stardom. In fact, the author poignantly limns an homage to creativity in all its forms: 'Simply stated, I was attracted to these special people, whom I saw as "creators," fashioning their own worlds'…Curto's reminiscence is a delightful experience, easy though intriguing, a rare literary combination. A captivating tour of a lawyer's encounters with creative genius."

—*Kirkus Reviews*

For my five grandsons:

Tyler

Julian

Oliver

Trevor

and

Paul

To whom much is given, much is expected.

TABLE OF CONTENTS

FOREWORD

When he was seven years old, Tony Curto moved from the friendly environs of Brooklyn to New Hyde Park on the edge of suburban Long Island. Civilization seemed distant and the local stores were a half-mile away. He was the only Italian kid on the block. "I gave some bruises and received some in return," he explains now, at age 85, in *A Mind of Their Own*, his second book.

When the older boys next door became a problem, he developed a new approach that worked—he bit them. Even as a child, Tony Curto was an astute observer of human behavior. And later as a lawyer, he fine-tuned his boyhood strategy. "The way to stop an opponent often did not require a legal fistfight," he writes. "Just a sharp bite."

Curto, who attended Rutgers University and New York Law School and was a star lacrosse player, entered the field of commercial law, working mostly outside the courtroom. The boardrooms and conference rooms of commercial law suited him. As he explains, "I did not like to be under any authority other than my client."

His clients exemplified his passion for the law—and something more. They had the courage of their convictions—and held fast to them despite the odds.

In *A Mind of Their Own*, Curto tells the stories of some of these clients who touched his life by following their own paths and principles. They range from financier Bernard Baruch and Soviet dissident Alexsandr Solzhenitsyn to star professional football player Freeman McNeil and entrepreneur Joy Mangano, a divorced Long Island mother of three who invented a mop that brought her fame and fortune.

Curto sees their fighting spirit as courage. At the age of 95, Baruch, who spent a lifeline advising presidents and politicians, fought to preserve a pristine stretch of South Carolina as an environmental education and research center. A Nobel Prize winner, Solzhenitsyn fought a repressive Soviet regime with his intellect and his words. New York Jets running back McNeil fought the National Football League as lead plaintiff in an antitrust lawsuit that helped earn players the right of free agency. And Mangano never wavered in her fight to build her company, then save it, and eventually sell it—and came away with 10 million dollars for her moxie.

Then there was Christian Lopez, a 23-year-old baseball fan whose only claim to fame was that he was fortunate enough to be in the stands when Yankee shortstop Derek Jeter homered for his 3,000th hit. Christian caught the ball in the third inning of the game against the Tampa Bay Rays—and later returned it to Jeter. "Mr. Jeter," he said simply, "this is your ball and I would like you to have it."

Curto wrote a letter to Christian, including a donation to honor his actions and pay some of his student loans, and later counseled him when the young man's accountant worried that the IRS would put a gift tax on the ball. The attorney still thinks of the fan, who could have sold the ball for hundreds of thousands but didn't factor financial reward into his calculations. "He was just a kid and he delivered," Curto writes. For Tony Curto, these people, as disparate as they may seem, are heroes. They're fueled by a special kind of courage that he searches for and seeks to define. These are the people who have inspired him – and whom he hopes will inspire his readers.

—*Harvey Aronson*, *best-selling author, former award-winning Newsday columnist and a member of the founding faculty of the School of Journalism at Stony Brook University.*

PREFACE

Many writers know exactly where they want to go—or think they do. When I started to write this book, I thought it would be about some remarkable people and their stories, of which I was a part. Now that the book is completed, I am somewhat surprised to see where these stories took me. It turns out, they reveal a lot more about me than I ever realized or intended to disclose.

In many ways, I practiced law in a fairly conventional way, with one exception: I wanted to be near the creative forces I saw in certain individuals. I don't know how I got this way, but as I look back it's been with me all my life and has shaped many of my interests and decisions. I always wanted to be part of something bigger and better than I was. Simply stated, I was attracted to these special people whom I saw as "creators," fashioning their own worlds. I have always thought that artists and entrepreneurs, like God, create, while explorers and scientists discover. The difference to me is profound.

All these stories have a common thread, which was unseen to me as I was living through them. The thread is the unique individuals whose goals captured my imagination and compelled me to support them. These people have defined my legal life.

This discovery was the unexpected reward for writing this book, for which I am most grateful.

1

Beginnings

This book is about a life—my life as a lawyer. But it's not just about my life. It's about the extraordinary people I got to work with along the way, a journey of six decades practicing law in New York and in far-flung places I never imagined I would find myself. You see, I discovered early on that while I loved the law, I was not enamored with the courtroom. What I *really* loved was the entrepreneurial spirit of America, and I recognized that I had an eye and ear for people who were a cut above, who had bold ideas. My generation was not part of the Greatest Generation; we accreted all the benefits with none of the sacrifices. But I was fortunate enough to represent and support a wide range of special clients, people I think of as heroes, whatever their generation.

This book is about these people and the times we lived in—how those times affected me, and how I affected those times and tried to advance the goals and accomplishments of remarkable individuals who represent the greatest aspirations our nation can offer.

* * *

I was born in 1936. My first home was at 38 Hart Street in Brooklyn, New York, where the Dodgers played on the edge of Bedford-Stuyvesant, one block away from where Barbra Streisand lived.

My earliest memories were of pushcarts and horse-drawn wagons selling fruit, vegetables and fresh fish that made routine stops at my stoop. The horse manure in the streets was harvested by women who would shovel it into boxes and use it for fertilizer in their gardens. I lived in a three-story brownstone surrounded by three-story homes like mine. It was a predominantly Jewish and Italian neighborhood. Everybody knew everybody else's business—and what they were eating for dinner. The women were "stay-at-home moms," long before the phrase was invented, and they managed to watch all the children who played in the streets. None of us escaped their all-seeing eyes.

On our block, we played stickball, hockey and hopscotch, roller skated, jumped rope, burned Christmas trees and cooked potatoes. When our fathers came home from work, we would spot them as they turned the corner, and we made a quick mental calculation as to whether we were going to be disciplined for the day's transgressions.

Moma's was the local grocery store where we would be sent to buy milk and other items, usually with fifty cents. The owner added the bill on the outside of the brown paper bag, which served as our receipt. He was faster than any adding machine, and my mom said she never saw him make a mistake.

The candy store, Glick's, sold us our toys, ushering in a new season every year. Yo-yos, comic books, baseball cards, cap pistols and kites: There was always something new and exciting that got us to beg money from our moms. We made scooters out of orange crates, and we separated our old roller skates into front and back parts and nailed them to two-byfours. Everything had a purpose; it was used until it broke or wore out.

Every so often an enterprising guy would show up on the street with a pony, a western saddle and a cowboy hat. Chaps were affixed to the saddle so that they could be flipped over our legs, and for a brief, thrilling moment all the kids in the neighborhood would become cowboys in the Old West. He took our pictures and sold them to our parents—my sister and I still have them in our homes.

Whenever we could find some dirt in our beloved Brooklyn that was not yet paved over, we played mumblety-peg with our pocketknives. The object of the game was to throw our knives into a box that we had drawn on the ground and divided into several parts. The winner was the one who stuck his knife in the most territory within the box.

We matched cards of our favorite baseball players for hours. Little did we know that years later, some of those cards would be worth tens of thousands of dollars, as would the comic books we traded. We played marbles with "shinies" and "k bollers." Our thumbs hurt from flicking marbles into the holes we had cut out in cheese boxes. The winner was able to shoot all of his marbles into the box. If you missed, you lost your turn.

In the summer, ice cream trucks came to our neighborhood. We'd hear their bells from blocks away, and so forewarned, we had time to scramble for ice cream money.

From time to time, trucks came to our front doors and delivered loads of coal, which had to be sluiced into our basements and then shoveled into the bins by our fathers when they came home from work. The coal dust would remain on the sidewalk for several days after each delivery. Every morning and evening in the winter, my father tended to the fire so that our family and the tenants would have heat and hot water. All the families in the neighborhood rented out the upstairs of their homes, unless they were occupied by their extended families. We had electricity and indoor plumbing and an ice box—no refrigerators yet—for the ice that was delivered regularly to our home, as was the milk.

My earliest recollection of a meaningful person in my life was Lila Green, our part-time black maid. My enterprising mother had negotiated for Lila after I was born. Knowing that my dad, who already had a daughter, wanted a son, she struck a bargain: My dad got me; my mom got Lila Green.

I vividly remember Lila coming into my life. Even today, I can close my eyes and recall her special smell, since I hugged her daily. In my early childhood she would tell me stories filled with lessons about right and wrong—what it meant to be a good boy. She would tell stories when she was ironing, and I would be enraptured by the images she conjured in my head. The troll always lurked under the bridge and would come to get me if I wasn't good, and the wolf was always at the door, also to be feared. I think much of my personality is grounded in those early stories told to me by a loving Lila Green.

Today Lila would be called a nanny (meanings of words seem to have changed lately). She worked to keep the house clean and bring order into our lives. But more important, having such a positive experience with Lila Green at an early age showed me that black people were very special in emotional and spiritual ways.

Years later, when I was in law school, I reflected on the significance of those days, and I was prompted to find Lila so I could tell her how important she had been to me. I went to her last address and found she had moved without leaving a forwarding address. I attempted to find her in other ways, but to no avail. I lost a very important piece of my life, and there will always be a hole because I never got to say good-bye. The lesson is simple: When somebody in your life is special, stay close.

I went to P.S. 54, an elementary school at the end of my block. I felt some apprehensiveness those first few days, but my fears subsided when I met my first teacher, who was beautiful and black and looked like Vanessa Williams with the comforting warmth of Lila Green. While those days are now mostly a blur, I do have a few recollections. I remember we had rest periods and were served small cartons of milk. I also remember eating the white paste that we used in class to display our drawings.

My life was disrupted by World War II. I sensed a change in the tone of my parents' conversations; they were not as sure of their future as they had been. My father was too young for World War I, unlike his brother Frank, who died in Europe, and he was too old to serve in World War II. This fortuitous generational cycle continued for me (I was too young for the Korean War, too old for the Vietnam War) and then for my only son. Unfortunately, I observed many of my friends and family members serving in all our wars during the last century, often making great sacrifices.

Even though my father remained at home, things were clearly different. When the sirens blew, my mother went into the night with an air raid warden hat on her head, flashlight and armband, ordering people to douse their lights so that the city would not be easily targeted by German bombers. Although I could barely write, I had a pen pal, a girl in England. Exciting! She seemed so far away on the map, but the letters of thanks for the packages and letters we sent were real.

As the war progressed, we were required to collect all sorts of essential materials in support of the war effort. President Franklin Roosevelt appointed the prominent financier

Bernard Baruch to be the country's industrial czar, in charge of maximizing production and efficiencies to marshal the power of our entire economy. This was a job Baruch had discharged admirably in World War I. Bacon fat, newspapers and scrap metals were regularly stored for pickup. When we went grocery shopping, we had to show our ration books, which limited what we could buy.

In 1943 my dad's company moved from Brooklyn to Lake Success, Long Island, a small village east of New York City, so we found a new home in nearby New Hyde Park. I had to give up my secret hiding place in the stoop behind our brownstone where I put my precious belongings. It was a nifty spot; nobody knew about it.

My new address, 74 Gerard Avenue, was a seismic shift from Brooklyn. (I never did find a new hiding spot.) In those days Long Island was more rural than might be imagined today, with an abundance of farms. New Hyde Park, with its early tract housing, was at the leading edge of the suburban sprawl later exemplified by Levittown. There were fields surrounding our house on almost all sides, and most of the homes were brand new. Mowing lawns, shoveling snow and weeding were all new chores—none of which I liked.

Nothing was nearby. Everything was a good hike away for a little seven-year-old guy. The stores, which my mother sent me to from time to time, were less than half a mile from our house, but in cold and wet weather these trips were a chore. A bicycle became a necessity. When I got my first bike, I felt as if the world had opened up to me—a feeling I had again years later, when I got my first car.

In the field behind our house, Army soldiers were stationed. There were barracks from which they launched dirigibles to protect military installations and factories near us. It was a scary sight. My mother prepared food that I brought to them to make them feel more at home. One day, when all my family members were home, we heard cannon fire in the distance. I never did find out whether this was a military exercise or some actual conflict. There were always rumors that German U-boats had landed spies on our shores—one of which turned out to be true, although their mission upon landing on Long's Island's East End proved unsuccessful.

We had moved into a neighborhood that my mother called "American." The families were Irish, English, Swedish, German and who knows what else. Being the new kid on the block and the only Italian, I immediately had to deal with prejudice and bullying. Sometimes things got a little rough and tumble. I navigated this fairly well; I gave some bruises and received some in return. No adults stepped in to arbitrate the fairness or lack thereof. It was kids figuring out how to get along with kids.

I particularly remember a confrontation with our neighbor's sons, who were constantly harassing me. My response: I bit them. When their mother later asked me why, I explained that I wanted them to stop them from bothering me. I wasn't interested in beating them; I just wanted them to stop. They never bothered me again. And years later, I realized that many of these early experiences actually prepared me well for life. Clearly, children did not like being bitten. But neither do adults, whether by a dog or by another adult. I took that observation into the practice of law, recognizing that the way to stop an opponent often did not require a legal fistfight; just a sharp bite.

I attended New Hyde Park Grammar School, and it was there that I had my first growing-up experience outside my family. Mr. Mondy, an ex-Marine and survivor of Iwo Jima, took on the burden of shaping my character. I was a poor student until seventh grade, when I had Mr. Mondy for science and math classes. I got a big dose of him (he was also my homeroom teacher), and he would regularly bring me down to the janitor's room in the basement of the school and discipline me with a radiator brush on my backside. In short order, my grades in math and science skyrocketed and I gained confidence. I was regularly disciplined the same way at home. I can't be certain that there wasn't a better way, but for me, it worked. It got my attention. And I performed.

Many of my memories of high school and college centered on team sports, lacrosse and football. I was captain of all the teams I played on, but the honor I most revered was being elected most valuable player of my high school teams by my teammates. I graduated from Sewanhaka High School in 1954 with the highest academic average of all varsity letter winners in my class.

I couldn't replicate those achievements at Rutgers. Everybody got bigger, stronger, faster and smarter, so I fell back into the pack. College was an unusual experience for the general student population in those days. Only a quarter of my graduating class from Sewanhaka went to college, and not all of them graduated. I was the first male child to go to college in my family. My father graduated from high school at age fifty-six and my mother never got past fourth grade. My sister also went to college, and my parents were extremely proud of both of us.

At the time, Rutgers was a small, private liberal arts college with a highly regarded engineering program and a reputation for being academically rigorous. Our graduating class had 800 students. Rutgers is now the State University of New Jersey, with more than 70,000 students. If I were applying today, I would never choose Rutgers. I wanted to be part of a small community of students.

I didn't adjust well to this community—not for a while, at least. I was homesick and not prepared to be on my own. I hadn't learned the discipline necessary to perform well in higher education. I made a number of bad decisions, including joining the wrong fraternity and falling in with a group of guys who didn't care much for academics but were good buddies for partying and going to the movies.

My freshman year I had a dorm-mate named Keir Dullea, who left one month into his first term. His roommate said he was unhappy; he wanted to be an actor, so he left for Hollywood. We didn't hear much about him until it was announced that he had gotten the lead part in the classic science fiction film *2001, A Space Odyssey*. Apparently, he got what he wanted out of college.

Another one of my buddies during freshman year was Charlie Marx, who had an Oldsmobile 98 convertible. In 1954 that was one heck of a car, and we used it to go to every movie in the state of New Jersey and date girls at Douglass College, our sister school across town. His first year Charlie managed to get an F in every course he took. I never heard of such an achievement, then or now. When he showed up sophomore year, I wondered how he got reinstated. He said his godfather had written a letter to the dean of the college. I later found out that Charlie's godfather was President Dwight D. Eisenhower—and that his father owned Marx Toys. Charlie left school halfway through the term, and I never heard from him again.

For the first three years of college, it seemed that I was always behind. When I got used to something, it changed, and I couldn't readily adapt to meet the next challenge. The decisions I made were usually bad. It wasn't till my senior year, after I moved out of the fraternity house and into the freshman dormitory, that I found some stability. I felt grown up compared to the freshmen I was living with. I went out for the lacrosse team and was elected captain and most valuable player on what some people thought was the best team in the history of Rutgers lacrosse. Of course, another team thought we were the *second* best.

My senior year gave me the confidence to make plans in line with my capabilities; finally, I was moving ahead. By the end of the year, I had decided I wanted to be a lawyer, although the thought of spending three more years in school was excruciating. I was never particularly interested in learning for learning's sake. I wanted to achieve particular goals, and learning was a necessary process to achieve those goals. I'm naturally inquisitive, but my level of inquiry had generally been superficial in areas I had no urgency to understand.

That would all change quickly. While I wanted to get out and do something, make money and be self-reliant, I knew I had to get through law school. I heard that New York Law School was offering a two-year program, day and night, with no summer vacations, and I could graduate in two years. That was just what the doctor (of law) ordered. Years later, I was gratified to learn that Judge Judy Sheindlin was also a graduate of New York Law School. The presiding judge on a highly acclaimed TV court show, Judge Judy became the most celebrated and financially successful lawyer ever to practice law in the United States—with a reported net worth of $420 million. And she was not just a celebrity; her view of justice would match my own philosophy, namely, that the current judicial system takes too long and costs too much, failing to reinforce the right principles for good human conduct. She meted out justice quickly and made complex issues simpler for all to understand.

At last, I saw my future. Let the games begin!

At New York Law I had the opportunity to learn lessons that I would use for the rest of my life. This was "directed learning," specific to a field that would be my pathway to independence, personal achievement and, I hoped, a lifetime of satisfaction. I enthusiastically started school with fifty other similarly motivated men and three women who wanted to finish school in two years instead of the usual three. More than half the class was Jewish. Some of them had jobs, and some of them were married with children. I admired these students, as I was a full-time student and knew how hard the studies were without these additional burdens. My classmates had a no-nonsense approach toward their life and aspirations. The competition was keen. The debates in class and in the hallways were contentious and argumentative, covering the gamut of law, politics, sports and every other topic of current interest. It was a wonderful training camp for the life that lay ahead of me. I found these encounters exhilarating, athletic—like my experiences playing team sports—and so I flourished.

On the first day of law school, I met a classmate who was clearly a person of substance, even as a student. When Robert Elkins opened his mouth, people listened. He garnered respect. Bob and I enjoyed many intense discussions during our time in school, and after we graduated and went our separate ways these discussions continued. There were long periods of non-communication, but when we met again, we would pick up where we had left off. Bob's standard opening comments were always calculated to make me feel guilty for not calling him. This was a familiar opening salvo; my mother used the same technique on me when I called her.

Bob relished standing in front of his classmates and going toe to toe with professors on the issue at hand. He never lost his cool, nor did he ever fail to make a salient point. Bob knew that the cases we were studying went to an appellate court at one time and their decisions were almost always split, with a minority and majority opinion being rendered. He knew the majority position, but he would often take the minority argument, comfortable knowing that some learned judges were on his side. Not surprisingly, Bob would go on to have a storied career as one of the most respected and successful trial lawyers in New Jersey.

The intensity of this two-year program made a lasting imprint on me. What a way to learn! A minimum of outside influences and a constant bombardment of legal principles, all in pursuit of one's life's work. Because we'd made a year-round commitment, nothing else got in the way of our absorbing the law and all its implications. It was boot camp, and many of the tenets of the law I learned remain with me till this day. Bob Elkins and I shared this experience; our friendship would last more than fifty years.

Along the way, I took courses with two nationally prominent professors. One was Roy Cohn, who was counsel to Senator Joseph McCarthy and to the notorious U.S. House Un-American Activities Committee, which was charged with ferreting out alleged communists in our country's institutions. Cohn was an extraordinary individual. He graduated law school and passed the bar before reaching the age of twenty, and he was only in his late twenties when he went to work for McCarthy. He was a central figure in those historic House committee hearings where a number of prominent people were falsely accused of being un-American and instruments of the Russian government.

When he returned to private practice, Cohn came to New York Law School to teach several courses. He would arrive in a limousine, sporting a glowing winter tan—no briefcase, papers or textbooks. Sitting in front of us, he would deliver lectures on criminal law for three straight hours, without notes. It was a *tour de force*. He exhibited self-assurance and knowledge that were overwhelming, leaving little room for alternative thinking. And yet, his demeanor in the classroom was far from the intimidating presence he exhibited in a courtroom or before Congress. He was instructional and friendly—even a bit shy—and relatively easy to approach.

We did not know at that time that he was gay, but we knew he was brilliant, and we accepted his behavioral quirks the way you would accept those of a gifted artist.

Another nationally prominent professor was William Kunstler. In our first year, when he taught real property law, his dress and manner were Ivy league from head to toe: tweed jacket, blue shirt with a button-down collar and the customary foulard tie. He was neatly groomed, short hair always brushed. We'd often see him on television giving his opinion about some current legal topic. In fact, he was on TV so frequently that we called him TV Bill.

But when he entered the classroom the next year, we were dumbfounded. His hair had grown out into an Afro and he appeared totally disheveled. This was a new William Kunstler; we called him Wild Bill. The change was so dramatic that we had difficulty catching up to this new persona. He was entirely radicalized, anti-authority and anti-institutional, and using his ample legal skills, he took up the cudgels for those protesting the government at every turn. He developed an extraordinary reputation as a champion of this generation's radicals, representing groups such as the Black Panthers and underground revolutionaries who bombed big banks and multinational corporations. For the rest of his life, Kunstler continued to make his mark defending individuals whose rights and civil liberties, he alleged, had been abridged by the Establishment. We never were sure what triggered these dramatic changes (had Dr. Timothy Leary enticed him into a mind-bending acid trip?), but as with Roy Cohn, William Kunstler showed us a style of law that we had never seen before.

In the beginning of my second year, another event took place that would shape my legal destiny. It was the kind of serendipity that I was lucky enough to encounter much of my career. The dean of New York Law School was Daniel

Gutman, who had served in Albany as Governor Averill Harriman's administrative aide. Every other year he would teach the school's course in evidence, and as fate would have it, during one of his teaching years, he was my professor. He looked like most of the professors: well groomed, with an air of academic distinction. As he started to outline the course for the coming year, he suddenly interrupted his presentation. Looking at the roster of names before him, he asked, "Who is Mr. Curto?" I raised my hand, and he asked me to see him after class.

I had no idea of why he had singled me out, but I presented myself as he had requested. He asked whether I had a relative named Curto who was a legislative leader in Albany representing the city of Buffalo. I told him I had no knowledge of such a relative, but he went on to describe this Curto as his best friend in Albany, with whom he enjoyed many productive and interesting hours.

Well, you didn't have to be a rocket scientist to realize that of the roughly fifty students in the course, he would be sure to remember my name, so I'd better come prepared. I was right. From time to time, when Gutman asked a question that seemed to stymie the class, he would call out, "Mr. Curto, do you know the answer?" More often than not, I did. My preparation paid off, and this added pressure probably helped me shine a bit brighter.

As the second year drew to a close, the entire class was trying to line up jobs. I had no contacts in the profession, and I didn't know where to start. Enter Dean Gutman. He told me there was a Madison Avenue law firm by the name of Buhler, King & Buhler that was looking for a young law clerk at sixty dollars a week. The firm had a fine reputation, providing services comprising both tax and legal advice to a group of clients of national and international fame. The dean wrote a glowing letter of recommendation, and the senior partner of the firm, Nelson Buhler, requested that I come in for an interview. I joined the firm right out of law school and had a chance to work with a roster of star clients such as Bernard Baruch, Douglas Fairbanks Jr., Gene Tunney, Jane Pauley, Gary Trudeau, Hank Ketchum, Harrison Salisbury and David Atkinson, as well as the presidents of all three major television networks at the time, along with an assortment of other TV and theatrical personalities This was an opportunity of a lifetime, and my first exposure to the potential magic of commercial law that was to repeat itself regularly during the course of my professional life.

Every successful person has to find out what his or her niche is, and I found mine. I was exactly where I wanted to be: outside the courtroom whenever possible, with minimum rules. I had a talent for understanding the facts of a case, the financial needs of the parties and the psychology that would be the glue to hold the deal together. Many of my partners and contemporaries thought that I could be a wonderful trial lawyer, but they missed a nuance of my talent—that I did not like be under any authority, other than that of my client.

After many years of intensive trial work, my friend Bob Elkins complained that the legal shenanigans common in today's courtrooms had robbed him of his youthful innocence. He marveled at my continued enthusiasm and wondered how I remained upbeat. The reason was simple. Bob's work was always about one side winning and the other side losing. I, on the other hand, worked in the commercial field, negotiating deals, buying and selling assets and companies. Clients who left the table after a deal had been struck generally felt that they got what they wanted and that the process was fair. This was the place I felt most comfortable—the least amount of legal structure, no judge to pander to or jury to win over. My adversary was on the other side of the table, and while it wasn't always easy, I was skilled at negotiating business matters to their conclusion, giving and taking in order to accommodate specific business needs.

I was born into the Golden Age of lawyerdom, and I was eager to take on professional life. At an early age, I learned from my mother always to look to the future. No matter my achievement, she would say, "Never mind that, that's over. What are you thinking about next?"

With the right preparation and a little luck, life has a way of rewarding you, especially if you live in a country like the United States at the right time. Branch Rickey, the great Brooklyn Dodgers general manager who signed Jackie Robinson, once said that luck is the residue of design.

I can't argue with that.

2

Bernard Baruch

A tap on the nose, a thorny problem resolved—
and a brilliant legacy fulfilled

By the time he was thirty, Bernard M. Baruch was already a self-made multimillionaire—his is the classic story of a hard-working young man who used his extraordinary entrepreneurial talent to realize the American dream.

Born in 1870, Baruch was the son of a Sephardic Jewish mother, Belle Wolfe, and a German Jewish father, Simon Baruch, who immigrated to South Carolina at the age of fifteen. Simon Baruch worked as a bookkeeper before he began to study medicine, eventually earning a medical degree from what is now Virginia Commonwealth University. He began his career as a surgeon in the Confederate Army during the Civil War, treating wounded soldiers right on the battlefield. Following the Confederate defeat at Gettysburg, he stayed on for six weeks to treat the wounded before he was imprisoned for several months at Fort McHenry.

After the war, Simon Baruch continued practicing medicine in South Carolina for sixteen years. He advocated giving the smallpox vaccination to children, served as president of the South Carolina Medical Association and was chairman of what would become the South Carolina Department of Health and Environmental Control. Yet, despite Simon's service in the Confederate Army and his distinguished career as a physician, life in Camden, South Carolina, was still a largely isolating existence for young Bernard Baruch and his family. Jewish families were rare in the South, and the prominent social clubs—country clubs, yacht clubs, golf clubs—all had restrictions that locked out Jewish members.

When Bernard was eleven, Simon Baruch moved his wife and four sons to New York City. He became an active public health advocate and scholar, known for his pioneering work in hydrotherapy, the use of clean water in rehabilitation therapies and the treatment of various ailments.

Young Bernard enrolled at the City College of New York. It was a time when Ivy League schools restricted enrollment to children of the wealthy Protestant establishment, and thousands of brilliant Jewish students attended City College—a free public institution—because they had no other option. City College became known as the poor man's Harvard; ten alumni from this era went on to win Nobel Prizes.

Graduating in 1889 at age nineteen, Baruch always maintained a close connection to his alma mater, and over the years he contributed substantial gifts to the college. In 1953, the School of Business and Civic Administration at City College was renamed the Bernard M. Baruch School of Business and Public Administration, and a few years later it became Baruch College, an independent four-year college, part of the City University of New York. Baruch is ranked among the nation's top colleges today, educating many working class and immigrant students from more than 160 countries.

While Bernard would write later that he often wished he "had not given up my earlier intention to study medicine," he ended taking a very different path—to the world of high finance on Wall Street. Starting out as an errand boy, he soon made partner at A. A. Housman & Company, but he then bought a seat on the New York Stock Exchange and became known as the "Lone Wolf of Wall Street," never again joining a large financial house. Other brokerages managed the accounts of outside clients, but Baruch seldom took on such clients. As he acquired great wealth, he remained a singular enterprise, an independent-minded person who managed his own investments from his Lower Broadway office.

Baruch was a brilliant observer of economic events. By taking advantage of the invention of the long-distance wireless telegraph—developed by another notable entrepreneur, Guglielmo Marconi—Baruch made tens of millions of dollars engaging in international arbitrage. He would place orders for U.S. securities on the London Stock Exchange one day and sell them on the New York Exchange the next day, taking advantage of the price differences in different markets for the same asset, which he knew in advance.

When World War I broke out in Europe in 1914, Baruch realized that the war would mean a surge in demand for American products. He scored huge gains, repeatedly buying shares when the stock market declined in reaction to Allied defeats, then selling when the market surged in response to Allied victories.

When the United States entered World War I in 1917, Baruch was appointed chairman of the War Industries Board, which oversaw much of the U.S. economy. (To avoid conflicts of interest, Baruch ceased his trading activity, forgoing sizeable profits to serve his country.) For Baruch, that was the beginning of a distinguished career in public service. He became a national hero for his efficient work in helping the country mobilize for the war. After World War I ended, he was asked to join the U.S. delegation to the Versailles Peace Conference.

Over the next forty years, Baruch would serve as a key adviser to seven U.S. presidents, both Democrats and Republicans, from Woodrow Wilson to Dwight Eisenhower. During World War II, he remained a close adviser to President Franklin Roosevelt, and later, President Harry Truman appointed him as the U.S. representative to the United Nations Atomic Energy Commission. Baruch's ability to cross political lines was (and is!) almost unheard of. Once you were an adviser to Republicans, you were dead to Democrats—and the other way around. But Bernard Baruch won the respect of both parties; they understood how staunchly individual Baruch was, fully capable of serving both sides of the aisle.

When I first encountered Bernard Baruch in 1965, I was twenty-eight; he was ninety-five. At the time, I was a partner in the boutique Madison Avenue Law firm Buhler, King & Buhler, which had represented Baruch's late daughter, Belle W. Baruch.

Baruch had approached the U.S. Trust Company, the financial custodian of his fortune, looking for a law firm to guide him in formulating the family's charitable goals and setting up a suitable tax-exempt vehicle. U.S. Trust (now owned by Bank of America) was a venerable private bank for the wealthy. Its chairman, Hoyt Ammidon, and president, Charles Buick, recommended my firm, which specialized in estates, trusts and foundations.

Since I was just finishing a master's degree in taxation and had expertise in charitable foundations, I was tapped for the job. I knew Baruch was interested in creating a charitable trust in his daughter's name, but I had no inkling of the brilliant scheme he had in mind.

I would soon find out.

One spring morning, Baruch invited a small group of advisers and lawyers, along with their wives, to come to South Carolina to meet with him. The trip was a throwback in time—it was something the average person never got a glimpse of. We traveled in a private railroad car built to Baruch's specifications, including sleeping compartments, and staffed with a chef, a butler and maid service. It was a window into how the business elite traveled to and from New York's Pennsylvania Station in the early decades of the twentieth century—the equivalent of private jets used by today's super-rich CEOs, movie stars and rock bands.

It was also a reminder of how isolated the upper and lower classes were from each other, with a clear line of demarcation. The very wealthy socialized only with people of their own stature. They lived in their city brownstones and country estates, and they traveled between them on their own private railroad.

For Baruch, this lifestyle usually meant taking the train at midday from Penn Station, traveling overnight and being greeted the next morning in South Carolina, where he would be chauffeured to his sprawling estate known as Hobcaw Barony—16,000 acres of pristine land squeezed on a peninsula between Route 17 and the Atlantic Ocean, just south of Myrtle Beach. The local Native Americans called this land *hobcaw*, meaning "between the waters," and in the early eighteenth century it was one of ten colonial baronies bestowed by English King George I.

Baruch bought the property in 1905 as a place where he could "shake loose from Wall Street and go off to some quiet place," as he would write later in his autobiography, *Baruch /My Own Story*. During this era, Hobcaw offered "the finest duck hunting in the United States, with four rivers and a bay abounding in fish; vast stretches of almost primeval forest, and—no telephone." As we neared our destination, I began to wonder how I would relate to this world. My background was completely different. Here I was, a second-generation Italian-American who grew up living next to a busy street in Brooklyn, then on suburban Long Island. These people had to travel a mile up the driveway *just to get to their house*. Perhaps they thought engaging me was a substantial risk.

We were driven not to Hobcaw Barony but to Baruch's modest home in Georgetown County. During Baruch's later years, Hobcaw, with all its bedrooms and baths, was simply too much space for him, his nurse and cook. The Georgetown residence was more manageable—and it had a pool. Even Baruch's duplex apartment in Manhattan had a pool, which he swam in every day, accompanied by his nurse. He believed it contributed to his longevity—a lasting influence of his father's work in hydrotherapy.

After a lovely lunch, during which I almost drank from the finger bowl (I was saved from this *faux pas* by my partner's twelve-year-old daughter), I was ushered into Baruch's bedroom. The room temperature was in the high eighties. He was sitting upright in an elevated, beautifully made bed, wearing a dark blue, pinstriped, three-piece suit. He wore spectacles clipped to his nose, with a gold fob chain leading to a slit in his jacket lapel where a boutonniere would go. His watch was also adorned with a gold fob chain that tucked into his vest.

Even in bed, Baruch was an imposing figure. He had a fair complexion, with white hair—a striking contrast to his piercing, flinty blue eyes that were still youthful and intense. You could see the spirit of a young man in an older man's body. On closer inspection, I saw he had been reading a book with many dog-eared pages. It was his autobiography; apparently, it had been reread numerous times. (At the end of our meeting he would send me off with a signed copy.) As I took a seat in a wingback chair next to the bed, I felt uneasy. I wasn't sure why. Was I anxious, being in the presence of such an iconic figure, a financial titan and adviser to seven U.S. presidents? It took me a few minutes to realize that my discomfort was not so much mental as physical—I was sitting in chair of such oversized proportions that my feet could not touch the floor! As I looked around, I could see that *all* the furniture in the room was custom-made to accommodate Baruch's six-foot, four-inch frame. Baruch's estate was near the heart of the country's furniture industry, and clearly Baruch had taken full advantage of his fortuitous location.

When I regained my footing, literally, I began talking to Baruch about domicile issues, specifically the possibility of having to pay taxes in both New York and South Carolina, since he lived and owned property in both states. I knew that states were prone to consider people of wealth as domiciliaries, so they could impose taxes on them. And it was not unusual for people to be taxed in two or more states, because they were considered domiciliaries of each state. I was there to prevent that—to explain to Baruch how he could establish a single domicile, while still having multiple residences.

Baruch listened carefully and asked several questions. I had prepared an informal, hand-written declaration of domicile for him to sign, but Baruch was a person of formalities. "Shouldn't this be typed?" he asked. I said it should, eventually, but signing this paper now was just as legally enforceable, as long as its meaning was clear. He signed it.

All the while, I could sense Baruch sizing me up. After a few minutes of awkward silence, he indicated that he had another issue he wanted me to help him with. I knew that

Baruch had wanted to create a charitable trust involving Hobcaw Barony, but I was not prepared for what came next.

Years earlier, Baruch had given Hobcaw to his daughter, Belle, as an inducement to bring her back to the United States from Paris. Like her father, Belle was fiercely independent; she wanted to get out from under his shadow. So in the early 1920s, as she herself was entering her twenties, she went off to Paris, where she became caught up in the bohemian lifestyle of the "Lost Generation"—a constellation of some of the most influential artists and writers of the time. Hemingway, Stein, Picasso, Duchamp: Belle knew them all.

Belle also was a superb athlete who excelled as an equestrienne, and during the time she lived abroad, she won more than 300 prizes in France and other countries. But she loved the rugged, rolling forests and marshlands of Hobcaw. It was a sportsperson's paradise, and by the time Belle emerged as a young adult, she could outride, outshoot and outhunt many men in her elite social class.

When Belle returned to Hobcaw, she lived in a bucolic home Baruch had built for her, nestled in the pine and live oak trees covered in Spanish moss, not too far from the main road, U.S. Route 17. It was named Bellefield. For the rest of her life, Belle flourished at Hobcaw, living with her hunting dogs and her female life partner until she was stricken with cancer at age sixty-four. I had written Belle's last will and testament. Before she died, daughter and father agreed to put Hobcaw Barony into a private charitable trust, to be held in perpetuity. Preserving the unspoiled natural environment of Hobcaw would be Belle's legacy, but it would involve one final, surprising twist from her father.

As Baruch began to describe the issue requiring my help, he noted that next to Hobcaw Barony was another large property, the Arcadia Plantation; the two properties were separated by Route 17. Arcadia was owned by another old, prominent American family, the Vanderbilts. Originally bought by Isaac Emerson, founder of the Emerson Drug Company (makers of Bromo-Seltzer), Arcadia was passed along to Emerson's grandson, George Washington Vanderbilt III, whose scientific expeditions across the globe were often overshadowed by the lavish lifestyles of other members of the family.

Although there was no open hostility between the Baruchs and Vanderbilts, I could sense some subtle friction. The Vanderbilts were American royalty; the Baruchs were not. While the Vanderbilts recognized the financial success and wealth of Baruch, they never traveled in the same social circles. The Vanderbilts were a fixture of society everywhere. They hosted elegant parties, from their mansions on New York's Fifth Avenue to summer "cottages" in Newport and Ashville, North Carolina—the palatial Biltmore House. On Long Island, William Kissam Vanderbilt II, an auto-racing enthusiast, built the Vanderbilt Motor Parkway, a private road for cars only, so he could organize races without worrying about annoying residential intersections and horse manure.

Baruch went on to explain that Route 17, which generally ran north-south, swung westward as it ran into a two-lane bridge that crossed the Waccamaw River into Georgetown. The bridge, he said, was in severe disrepair, and the South Carolina Department of Transportation was going to replace it with a new four-lane bridge.

Here's where he zeroed in on the heart of the problem. His eyes narrowed. You see, he said, the new bridge could be built on either the north or the south side of the old bridge. If the new bridge was built south of the existing bridge, then Route 17 also would have to be redirected south of the current road. In that case, Baruch would end up owning both sides of the road frontage. If, however, the new bridge was built to the north of the existing road, then the Vanderbilts would have frontage on both sides of the road and Baruch's property would effectively be blocked for at least half a mile leading to the bridge.

That's *not* what Bernard Baruch wanted.

Then Baruch made his pitch: He wanted me to represent him in negotiations before the State of South Carolina, persuading transportation officials to construct the new bridge south of the existing structure, thus ensuring him road frontage on both sides of the road.

I was dumbfounded. Why would Baruch ask me to take on such a case? Clearly, he could take it to court; he had no shortage of financial resources. Besides, I wasn't a litigator. My area of expertise was tax and charitable foundation issues.

"Mr. Baruch," I said, grimly, "I am a young New York lawyer with no South Carolina connections. And I have a vowel at the end of my last name. I don't believe you will be well served by my representing your interests in this matter." I suggested that he hire a well-connected local firm.

Baruch did not accept my suggestion. Instead, he did something I've never forgotten: As he began to speak, he touched the side of his nose with his right index finger. I was transported back to my childhood, to the famous poem, "The Night Before Christmas." It's the moment, after everyone has gone to sleep, when the child encounters Saint Nicholas. Old St. Nick assures the child he has "nothing to dread"; then, "laying his finger aside his nose," he gives a nod and up the chimney he goes. It was a gesture I would come to recognize in Baruch: Whenever he wanted to reveal some important secret, he would touch the side of his nose.

(Years later, I was reminded of this gesture from the movie *The Sting*. In the film, the con men duo, played by Paul Newman and Robert Redford, would touch the side of their noses as a secret signal when their part of the scheme was completed. It seemed as if this nose swiping had become a universal gesture, transcending culture and time.)

As Baruch touched his nose, he said, in barely more than a whisper, that he had a chip to play. When I met with the department of transportation, I should make them this offer: If they rebuilt the bridge and redirected the road as Baruch proposed, he would make sure that Hobcaw Barony became a major nonprofit educational foundation, in perpetuity, where environmental research could be conducted in collaboration with the public and private educational institutions of South Carolina.

Now I understood.

Baruch would lose some property as a result of the relocation of Route 17, but he would maintain direct access to the bridge. In return, the state would see a significant benefit from a trust that would ensure that Hobcaw would be transformed into an outdoor laboratory for all of South Carolina's schools. This was not just any estate. It was an immense tract of undisturbed land right on the Atlantic coastline, which would eventually be dotted with busy resort communities. It contained every common ecosystem found on the Carolina coast, so it had the potential to become an unparalleled site for comprehensive research in the environmental sciences.

Hobcaw had never been developed; now it never would be.

I nodded. "Yes, I can do this," I said.

Several weeks later, I met with state officials and spent a good deal of time laying out Baruch's deal: The state would locate the new bridge and reroute Route 17 as Baruch proposed, and in return the citizens of South Carolina would receive a lasting gift—a unique research center dedicated the burgeoning field of environmental sciences.

In the end, our argument carried the day. I was able to secure a favorable settlement on Baruch's behalf, and the Belle W. Baruch Foundation was established.

Looking back on the negotiation, I've come to appreciate Baruch's scheme as much more than a simple *quid pro quo*. He had an amazing entrepreneur's vision—and he had a plan, with all the pieces in place. From the outset, Baruch saw that in settling the issue of the bridge, he could fulfill his family's tax and estate planning needs while simultaneously serving the people of South Carolina. He understood that the area's universities could not boast the financial and cultural resources of the venerable urban institutions of the Northeast. But through Belle's foundation, local universities could establish their own *gravitas* with an unmatched natural resource, infused with the intellectual value of highly trained scientists, educators and historians.

There was one last piece to Baruch's visionary plan: It was a way for him to tweak the formidable Vanderbilts. In getting state officials to agree to his Route 17 bridge proposal, Baruch effectively blocked the Vanderbilt family from any counter-move, since they would have to take legal action against a charitable trust, rarely a productive effort. It was important for Baruch not to be outmaneuvered by the Vanderbilts. I believe that in some deep, unspoken way he was still responding to being kept out of the social circles of South Carolina. I don't know if the outcome settled a long-standing feud or fanned the flames, but Baruch was pleased with my results.

As Baruch noted in his autobiography, throughout his life he found himself confronted with the challenge of "disentangling the impersonal facts of a situation from the elements of human psychology." When new situations arise, he said, "some persons dig their heels dogmatically into the past and declare that we must hold rigidly to the old rules.

Others treat each new situation as if it requires a *de novo* approach, relying on trial and error as if the past had no value. To govern ourselves effectively, both these extremes must be rejected. The real problem is to know when to stand by the old truths and when to strike out in new, experimental ways."

The bridge/Belle foundation saga gave me a rare window into Baruch's efforts to navigate between the "old truths" and the "new, experimental ways." Bernard and his daughter had the foresight to preserve the wildness of Hobcaw Barony; originally known as conservationists, they were early joiners of the environmental protection movement that would escalate in the 1970s, just as the Myrtle Beach development boom began to change the coastline forever. At the same time, Baruch knew that he had to find ways to move forward through inevitable change. That's when his entrepreneurial instincts kicked in: It was not enough to foresee events; it was essential to put himself in a position to control them.

In the early days, the foundation's board of trustees, for whom I served as counsel, faced similar challenges in determining the direction of the organization. The general instructions were in the trust, but the board had to hammer out the specifics.

It was a passionate discussion. There were two main factions. One faction wanted to proactively manage Hobcaw as an enterprising farm and facility. The second faction wanted to take a more restrained approach, preserving the land as a sanctuary in its natural state. Ultimately, the more restrained, custodial approach won out. The board choose to keep the land pristine, recognizing that by maintaining such a large ecosystem of woodlands and oceanfront habitats, the foundation would enable researchers to do comprehensive environmental studies that might otherwise not be possible.

Although the foundation was under the control of five trustees at the time, the board wanted to establish an advisory committee. Several people who were offered positions accepted them, including New York City Mayor John Lindsay, the film actor and producer Douglas Fairbanks Jr., and Howard Rusk, a prominent physician and brother of Dean Rusk, Secretary of State under President John F. Kennedy.

Surprisingly, one person who declined the board's invitation was Baruch's close friend, Jimmy Byrnes. James F. Byrnes was among the most influential political figures in the south during the decades spanning the careers of John Calhoun and Lyndon B. Johnson. Byrnes was elected to the U. S. House of Representatives and the U.S. Senate, eventually succeeded by Strom Thurmond. Byrnes also served as Secretary of State and the one hundred fourth governor of South Carolina, and he had a brief stint as an associate justice on the U.S. Supreme Court.

The foundation board thought Governor Byrnes would be wonderful addition to the advisory committee, so I called him. After explaining the history and mission of the foundation, I asked Byrnes whether he would be interested in serving on the committee.

"Who's above the committee?" he asked.

"The trustees," I said. "The committee acts as a sounding board for the trustees."

"So," he said, "my job is to give the trustees ideas and *they're* the ones who make up their minds?"

The governor took a moment. Then, in his southern drawl, he said, "Sonnn... I learnt a long, long time ago never to accept a responsibility without the authority. Because that's the way you get things done. And I'm a person who gets things done."

The conversation was over. It was an important lesson about management that I never forgot.

For several years, I served as general counsel to the Baruch Foundation and had a chance to visit Hobcaw on numerous occasions. The spacious manor house that now graces the property is not the original frame building, which caught fire and burned to the ground during the family's annual Christmas gathering in 1929. The mansion was rebuilt a year later, in compliance with the building codes of New York City, with internal stairways completely surrounded with stone—no more wood.

The Georgian-style brick structure is still enormous, and over Baruch's lifetime it offered a luxurious respite for many guests, from political figures like Winston Churchill and FDR to investment banker Otto Kahn, Army General Omar Bradley, *Time* magazine publisher Henry Luce and actor Walter Huston. President Roosevelt "enjoyed his stay so much he did not want to leave," Baruch recalled in his autobiography. "He had come to Hobcaw tired and with a cough. He left tanned and in better health, as Admiral Ross McIntire, his physician, told me, than in many a year."

I've visited the bedrooms at Hobcaw where a number of notable guests stayed. While I didn't sleep in any of the beds, I did take time to lie in them with my back against the headboards, reflecting on men who had slept there and the meaning of their visits. I thought about FDR and Churchill, who visited with Baruch before the end of World War II—two political giants discussing the problems they could face after the war with one of the great financial and practical minds of the time. I realized that what these men were talking about then was exactly what the world was facing during my own visits to Hobcaw: the Cold War.

Some fifty years later, while I was driving from Long Island to Florida, I decided to pay an impromptu visit to Hobcaw Barony. I came to the entrance, where there had once been a small dirt road and a wooden gate that one had to get out of the car to open. Now, there was a gigantic welcome center that told the story of what was being done there, who was doing it and who created it. I introduced myself to the receptionist, and I told him what my relationship was to the foundation. He called the executive director and director of programs, who immediately came out to greet me. They knew who I was, and they promptly offered to take me on a royal tour of the premises.

Over the years Hobcaw Barony has truly grown into what Belle envisioned: a vibrant center for "teaching and/or research in forestry, marine biology, and the care and propagation of wildlife and flora and fauna in South Carolina." The Belle W. Baruch Foundation works hand in hand with the University of South Carolina's Belle W. Baruch Institute for Marine and Coastal Sciences and Clemson University's Belle W. Baruch Institute of Coastal Ecology & Forest Science. It hosts researchers from over fifty universities and research organizations around the world, and provides educational programs for thousands of students, from kindergarten to high school.

There are also more than seventy cultural sites preserved on the estate, including former slave cabins, which I recalled seeing during my early visits. The plantations in this area were once the second largest producers of "Carolina Gold" rice, and even after emancipation, many former slaves and their descendants remained on Low Country plantations and lived in former slave villages until after World War II.

On this last visit to Hobcaw, I went to lunch at the plantation house where the trustees were having a meeting. I was invited to join them. That afternoon they heard the story of what took place in the early days of the foundation from the only living person who was there from the beginning.

3

Harry Chapin

Reflections on the whirlwind life of a "perfect biophile"

Born on December 7, 1942—one year after Pearl Harbor—Harry Chapin was a musician, songwriter, playwright, philanthropist and humanitarian who was tragically killed at the age of thirty-eight in a fiery crash on the Long Island Expressway. Harry was a dynamic force in support of the arts and charitable organizations across the nation. He left an indelible imprint on the community where he lived, and a hole in the cultural landscape that has never been filled.

Aside from his artistic contributions, Harry's life's ambition was to eliminate world hunger. He believed we had the resources to accomplish this goal; we just lacked the willpower. No small task, to be sure, but Harry Chapin refused to be deterred!

Harry was an intense lover of life—what I called "a perfect biophile." When Harry moved, every part of his body

moved, like a Rube Goldberg contraption. His good friend
the famed actor Robert Redford—a noted political and
environmental activist himself—marveled that he never met
"anybody with the degree of energy and the degree of commitment all tied into one force like him." Harry committed
himself tirelessly in support of practically every organization
or social cause that crossed his path. He sang in over 150
concerts a year, and at least half of them were benefits for
charity.

There were only two people in my life I could never
say no to. One person was Monsignor Tom Hartman, the
Roman Catholic priest from Long Island who made up half
of the "God Squad." Father Tom, as he was known, and
Rabbi Marc Gellman were introduced to America by radio
shock jock icon Don Imus. The duo became household
names thanks to the success of a TV show they co-hosted
for twenty years that led to a nationally syndicated newspaper column.

The other person was Harry Chapin. I realized this in
the early 1970s when I was conscripted into Harry's army
of locals to support what he called the "three cultural pil-
lars of Long Island": dance, theater and music. Harry had
a dream of creating a Lincoln Center for all Long Islanders;
he spent an enormous amount of time and energy mobiliz-
ing the business community to build and support regional
cultural institutions like the Performing Arts Foundation,
a theater and an education program; the Eglevsky Ballet;
and the Long Island Philharmonic, a professional symphony
orchestra.

Harry's wife, Sandy, a teacher, a poet and also a songwriter, had gotten interested in becoming more involved in
their local arts community—and getting Harry involved as
well, particularly raising money for organizations badly in
need of funds. Sandy had heard of me as a "nickel-plated

celebrity" (my own epithet, stolen from the late *Newsday* columnist Ed Lowe). She wanted to bring me onto the council board, and Harry was stalking me, trying to set up a meeting. At the time, I was reluctant to join up because I knew what it would mean: more work and more fundraising squeezed into my already busy schedule.

I ducked him for as long as I could, but one day when I was at work, with my defenses down, I heard a commotion in the outer office. Then...vague sounds of music. When I opened the door there was Harry, singing to my entire staff, like the Pied Piper. He had me; there was no escape. From that day forward, I was part of Harry's army, supporting the cultural life of Long Island and points beyond. Who could resist Harry's noble mission to eliminate world hunger?

Not me.

Harry Chapin would become known as "America's troubadour," one of the most popular singers of the 1970s who wrote self-described "story songs"—kind of miniature movie narratives, usually about common folks with poignant tales to tell.

In the beginning, Harry's career was not so promising. Before I began working with him, Harry was playing in a band in Manhattan's Greenwich Village. It was the early seventies, the peak years of the Village folk scene. In 1971, his manager, Fred Kewley, booked the downstairs room at the Village Gate, costing Harry $400 a week. The room held about two hundred people, but the group often would be playing to an audience of ten. On weekends they were lucky to get a hundred people a night.

From time to time, Harry would stand outside the club and "hook" people into the room, trying desperately to fill the seats. He called music critics at *The New York Times* and talent scouts at record companies, sometimes pretending to be his own manager. (He got caught once.) When Harry

was first starting out "he tended to be his own best promoter," Sandy Chapin would recall years later. "He was very
assertive about getting out and meeting people and getting
people to know his music."

Harry Chapin grew up in a family of artists. His father,
James Chapin, was a well-known jazz drummer who played
with band leaders Tommy Dorsey and Woody Herman.
While a teenager, Harry began playing with his brothers,
Tom and Stephen, with their father sometimes joining them
on drums. Still, at age twenty-nine, Harry Chapin knew
that he was trying to succeed where most performers failed.
And if all else did fail, he could still go back to his first career
choice, filmmaking. Harry had originally intended to be a
documentary filmmaker. His uncle, Richard Leacock, was a
famed *cinema verité* filmmaker, and Harry had worked for a
company called the Big Fights, which owned a large library
of classic boxing films. He had already directed a successful
documentary, *Legendary Champions*, which was nominated
for an Academy Award.

What followed next was one of those miraculous show
business stories that could have been a movie script. One
night, while singing at the Village Gate, Harry was discovered by a young talent scout for Elektra Records, Ann Purtill, who had never signed a major artist. During the first
five weeks at the Gate, the band under Harry's direction had
come together as a polished act. Ann was knocked out by
the band and Harry himself, especially when he introduced
his new song "Taxi." Purtill also knew that six other major
record companies had begun to show interest in Harry.

Ann tried to persuade her boss, Jac Holtzman, the owner
of Elektra, to sign Harry, but Holtzman was not as taken
with Chapin as Ann was. Ann didn't give up, and finally,
as a show of respect for his employee's intuition, Holtzman
offered Harry an advance of $3,500. (Carly Simon's origi-

nal advance was also $3,500.) Harry and Fred Kewley were ecstatic.

But that was just the beginning of a ten-day bidding war that stunned the music world. In the fall of 1971, a talent scout with Columbia Records saw Chapin perform at the Village Gate and told his boss, Clive Davis, about him. Davis loved Harry's story songs and offered him an advance of $5,000. These two industry giants, Holtzman and Davis, were good friends—but also fierce competitors.

Holtzman countered Davis's offer with $7,500—and then, after listening to "Taxi" while driving down the California coast, he raised his offer to $15,000. Davis doubled the offer—$30,000. Holzman came back with $25,000, knowing that Harry was looking to work with a smaller company. Davis countered with $50,000. Holtzman: $40,000. Then Davis again: $80,000. Finally, Harry agreed to an extraordinary multiyear contract from Holtzman worth more than $600,000. It was the biggest deal in Elektra's history, including nine albums and free studio time—unheard of at the time.

"For the first time in my life," Harry exclaimed, "I believed in capitalism!"

Over the next decade, Harry would continue moving in a hundred different directions at once. Half of them were sheer folly. The remaining half, however, were worth the effort and often succeeded. At one point, I joined two friends, Peter Barry, the president of Hartman Systems in Huntington, and James Brady, managing partner of Arthur Andersen's Long Island office, to form a group we called BCC, which stood for "Break Chapin's Balls." We had an honorable mission, which was to try to harness this life force, Harry Chapin, and focus his priorities into three categories: family, career and charity. We failed, although not for lack of effort.

Harry released twelve albums, selling millions of copies worldwide. His fourteen singles all became hits, including the iconic "Taxi," "Cat's in the Cradle" (taken from a poem Sandy wrote), "W.O.L.D" and "Sequel." When "Taxi" was performed on *The Tonight Show with Johnny Carson*, the show received so many calls that Chapin was called back the next night—the first time in the show's history that had happened to a performer.

He wrote three Broadway shows, performing in one of them, *The Night that Made America Famous*, which garnered two Tony Award nominations. He wrote the score for a TV movie, *Mother and Daughter, the Loving War*.

No mountain was too high, no government office too impregnable for Harry to breach, usually under the strategic guidance of his wife, Sandy. Starting in the early 1970s, combating hunger—whether at the local level or worldwide—became Harry's main extramusical passion. With his friend Father Bill Ayres, a local radio and TV personality, Harry founded World Hunger Year. Known as WHY, the organization had an ambitious mission: to identify the root social and economic causes of hunger and support community-based solutions. Harry was a key participant in creating the Presidential Commission on World Hunger during President Jimmy Carter's term. Locally, he created Long Island Cares, aimed at addressing hunger and food insecurity in the region. And he organized and appeared in myriad benefit concerts for consumer, social and environmental issues.

Harry was once quoted as saying, "I think I've had the most social and political involvement of any singer-songwriter in America." Not surprisingly, most experts agreed. Some years later, he was posthumously awarded the Congressional Gold Medal, the highest honor bestowed by Congress.

I was doing double duty, practicing law in conventional ways and heading up the Huntington Arts Council and New York State Council for the Arts. In his business dealings, Harry was pretty much a one-man band and often negotiated many of his own contracts, but when it came time to get paid by the recording companies, he would often employ me to "shake the money tree."

Before I began officially representing Harry in contract negotiations, I witnessed one of those show-biz stories that catapulted his reputation to new heights. In 1980, I had traveled with Harry and his accountant to Beverly Hills, California, to meet with Elektra. We were lounging around the Beverly Hilton pool, preparing for a meeting with Elektra's comptroller, which I knew would be contentious—it was well known that record companies did not always meet their royalty obligations and required some pressure to see them through. We were an odd-looking trio, the accountant and I dressed in dark blue suits, white shirts with button-down collars, striped ties and Oxford black shoes, while Harry—and everybody else in Southern California—was dressed-down "cool."

As we were reviewing financial reports, the waiter, serving us Cokes at poolside, mentioned that Bruce Springsteen was staying at the hotel in the penthouse suite, five stories above us. Harry immediately put down his drink and financial records and stood up. Facing the façade of the hotel, he yelled, "Bruce! Bruce! Bruuuuce!" each time louder than before. Other guests started to look up to see what the commotion was, and then we saw a head peeking over the penthouse balcony. After a couple more shouts, the rest of Springsteen's body came into view and Harry yelled, "What are you doing for world hunger, Bruce?" I could tell that Bruce was taken aback by the ambush, but after a few awkward moments he agreed to join Harry's Army. And so, in addition to the money that we received through our dealings with Elektra's accountants, Harry got a commitment from Bruce Springsteen. The California trip was a doubly rousing success!

Then the unthinkable happened.

Just after noon on July 16, 1981, Harry Chapin was driving west on the Long Island Expressway in his daughter's blue Volkswagen Rabbit. Harry was going to give a concert that evening before 30,000 fans in Eisenhower Park. It was to be a benefit. Of course.

Chapin was driving about sixty-five miles an hour in the left lane when, apparently having car trouble, he put on his emergency flashers, slowed to fifteen miles an hour and veered into the center lane, nearly colliding with another car. He swerved left, then right again, desperately trying to get out of the way of other cars and onto the right shoulder, when a tractor-trailer owned by Supermarkets General rear-ended him, sending him flying to the side of the road. The fuel tank of Harry's Volkswagen ruptured and the car burst into flames.

At great personal risk, the truck driver cut Harry free from the seatbelt and, with the help of the passenger of another vehicle, dragged him from the burning car. They didn't know that they were trying to save a dead man. A police helicopter transported Harry to a hospital, but he had died almost instantly as a result of the rear-end collision.

The next week was a blur. The only thing I remember is being at Harry's graveside and singing, "All My Life's A Circle." All Long Island was stunned and devastated. Although born in Brooklyn, Harry had become synonymous with the Island. He was clearly one of us, and when he died, the entire Island mourned. One minute he was here and everywhere. The next minute he was gone.

In the ensuing months, Harry's family spent thousands of dollars trying to establish the proximate cause of his death. They retained experts from many disciplines—not often had so much work been done in preparation for an auto accident case.

Sandy Chapin abhorred the publicity she knew would come if a wrongful death action were brought against Volkswagen and the supermarkets chain. Harry had five children, two with Sandy and the three others from Sandy's previous marriage whom he had legally adopted. Sandy was fearful of opening up her family's life to public scrutiny. But after considerable anguish, the family agreed to my bringing a lawful death claim on behalf of Harry's estate, mostly for pragmatic considerations: Sandy was left with very modest financial means of support, largely because Harry had assigned his multimillion-dollar life insurance policy to World Hunger Year, securing its future in the event of his death—but not his family's.

As attorney for the Chapin family, I was to be responsible for keeping tight control of Harry's story and the narrative of the case. The days leading up to the trial were terribly hurtful to Sandy. Supermarkets General did not contest legal liability, even though Harry was driving without a license at the time of the accident. (Harry was too busy saving the world to pay a long string of traffic tickets, so his license had been suspended.)

I ended up filing a complaint for negligence against both Supermarkets General, the owner of the truck, and Volkswagen of America. Among other things, the suit alleged that Harry would have survived the accident if Volkswagen had engineered the car's seatbelt system more safely. The seatbelt mechanism Harry was using was unsafe—and the company knew it.

This was a case of an international auto giant against an international singing star's family—millions of dollars at stake, as well as reputations. It's one thing to prove another driver's negligence; it's quite another to take on the safety system of Volkswagen. If the case went against Volkswagen, the company could potentially be liable for all the cars out there that had these types of seatbelts and be forced to make improvements in all of them or face substantial claims for damages.

The Chapin family knew that Volkswagen would be a formidable opponent. A lawsuit against the company would result in years of legal fighting, and then, even if we won the first round, appeals could be filed, and we'd end up going back to trial. Still, the family felt a strong sense of social responsibility and wanted to get some meaningful benefits out of the death of Harry. Following in the footsteps of Ralph Nader, who detailed his campaign against the Corvair in his book *Unsafe at Any Speed,* the Chapins decided that this would be a battle to help make cars safer.

The critical issue was the design of the Rabbit's seatbelt system. The company had changed the seatbelt configuration in the Rabbit so that it only went over Chapin's shoulder, not his across his lap. The shoulder strap Harry was wearing was effective in stopping injuries from front-end crashes—it prevented the body from smashing into the steering wheel. But the lap seatbelt, our experts told us, was essential in keeping the driver in his seat if the vehicle was hit from behind.

Because there was no lap belt in the Volkswagen model Harry was driving, we believed that when he was hit from behind his head ramped upward, hitting the roof with such force that it caused his torso to violently snap backward. His aorta ruptured; he instantly lost blood pressure and consciousness and died. Our case was strong, but the family knew it would be contested on every point—the counsel for Volkswagen was a seasoned litigator. Before the trial started, therefore, the Chapin family decided to drop Volkswagen as a defendant; the road was too long and uncertain and the costs too high. They decided to focus instead on Supermarkets General, where we had a better chance to expedite the case and be fairly certain that there wouldn't be further litigation.

Since the trial was only about damages, not liability, we concentrated on Harry's life expectancy and the longevity of his earnings. Multiple experts were retained to make projections of revenues Harry would have earned during his performing life if he had not died in the accident. We needed expert opinions concerning Harry's career: How durable was his talent? In order to demonstrate Harry's durability, I needed to have qualified experts to testify.

Sandy contacted two superstar performers who were also among Harry's close friends, Kenny Rogers and Harry Belafonte. They enthusiastically agreed to come to the aid of the Chapin family, testifying in support of Harry's enduring artistic talents. Given their hectic schedules, I prepped their testimony in the taxi on the way to the Southern District Federal Court in Brooklyn. The courtroom was visibly excited to have such celebrities present, but what set off an even greater buzz was what was happening in the courtroom next door.

In the adjacent chamber, the murder trial of the notorious Gambino family crime boss, John Gotti Jr., was being heard by Judge Eugene Nickerson, who had been Nassau County executive and was a well-known public persona himself. This was a high-profile FBI case, aimed at finally bringing down "Teflon Don" Gotti, who had managed to evade convictions in several previous cases. The star of this show was Salvatore "Sammy The Bull" Gravano, a former underboss of the Gambino family, who had agreed to testify against his flamboyant former boss in a deal where he confessed involvement in nineteen murders.

The courtroom and halls were loaded with press and curious observers. When the trials were recessed, members of our legal team along with our star witnesses would commingle with the defendants and their team—as well as that unusual entourage from Brooklyn, known for very different talents. It was an odd scene, to say the least. It was astounding to witness the "singing" of Sammy the Bull in one courtroom next to the chorus of Kenny Rogers and Harry Belafonte, filling our courtroom with storied songs. The following day, one New York tabloid ran the wry headline "Song Birds."

Seven years after Harry's death, thanks to my trial lawyer partners Jerry Sullivan and Ted Friedman, we were finally successful in obtaining a jury award of $10.57 million, which was split among Sandy and the five children.

It's been almost forty years since Harry's death, but he is still an enduring presence . The Harry Chapin Foundation, led by Sandy, continues to support organizations that help underprivileged people around the country become self-sufficient. World Hunger Year—now Why Hunger—is supporting sustainable, grassroots solutions and training programs that help community members grow their own food. And Long Island Cares continues to strive for a hunger-free Long Island.

Harry's remains lie on a hill in the Huntington Rural Cemetery; the epitaph on his tombstone is taken from his song "I Wonder What Would Happen to This World":

Oh, if a man tried
To take his time on earth
And prove before he died
What one man's life could be worth
I wonder what would happen
To this world.

4

Aleksandr Solzhenitsyn

The secret, high-risk scheme that brought the works of a Russian literary giant to the West

Any student of Russian literature today knows the name Aleksandr Isayevich Solzhenitsyn. Along with literary giants like Tolstoy, Pushkin, Chekhov, Dostoyevsky and Nabokov, Solzhenitsyn has an indisputable place in the pantheon of the greatest Russian authors of all time. A Nobel Prize winner and celebrated dissident, Solzhenitsyn exposed the Soviet government's prison camp system through literary works such as *The Gulag Archipelago*.

While Solzhenitsyn's writing is now a fixture in academia, how many students know that his works might never have appeared in our libraries, bookstores and classrooms? It was a perilously close call! And how many people today know the inside story of how Solzhenitsyn's works got past the oppressive Soviet censorship during the Cold War? It is a story of a small, dedicated group of Americans that I joined in the mid-1960s, who played a pivotal role in a high-risk, international scheme that secretly conveyed the works of Aleksandr Solzhenitsyn to the West. It is a story well worth telling.

The saga began, inauspiciously, in an Iowa cornfield. It was a September day in 1959—at the height of the Cold War—and Nikita Khrushchev, the brash premier of the Soviet Union, was on a state visit to the United States, the first by a Soviet leader. Khrushchev had come to Iowa at the invitation of Roswell Garst, a well-known seed-corn expert, in search of agricultural innovations that he could take back with him to better feed his people. (The visit convinced him to plant vast fields of corn throughout his country, even in cold regions with short growing seasons where it couldn't ripen fully but would ripen enough for animal feed.)

But on that day, Harrison Salisbury, who was among the throng of reporters covering the visit, was interested in more than corn: He confronted the Russian premier, challenging him on the freedom of artists in the Soviet Union. Harrison was a widely known correspondent for *The New York Times* who had won a Pulitzer Prize for a series of articles he wrote after serving as the *Times*'s Moscow Bureau chief. He asserted that the Soviet Union controlled its artists by refusing to be a signatory under the Berne Convention for the Protection of Literary and Artistic Works, an international agreement governing copyright protection, adopted in Berne, Switzerland, in 1886.

The lack of international treaty protection meant that all Russian texts shared with third parties, whether in the Soviet Union or elsewhere, were deemed to be in the public domain. Russian writers could not secure copyright protection, and publishers could not secure exclusivity rights over such works. Once a manuscript left the author's hands, they had no authority over its publication. In short, the refusal by the Soviet Union to adopt the Berne Treaty was a diabolical move aimed at crushing any independent artistic endeavors. Further, because the writings of Solzhenitsyn and others could not be widely disseminated, it stifled worldwide criticism of the Russian regime.

Since no publisher in the West could secure the exclusive right to publish a Russian author, there was no financial gain in promoting Soviet literary works. Realistically, no grandscale publication could emerge from the Soviet Union. The works that *did* manage to get smuggled out lacked literary significance and commercial value. They were attributed to hackneyed anti-Soviet dissidents—a tactic adopted repeatedly by the government in its effort to discredit the authenticity and value of these works. Their translations had been butchered by quick-buck publishers, since established publishing houses refrained from assuming their usual role.

One of Solzhenitsyn's early works, for example, *One Day in the Life of Ivan Denisovich,* initially made its way into the Moscow literary journal *Novy Mir* in 1962. It was authorized by Khrushchev (with some censorship), who gambled that the novel's publication would help advance his campaign of de-Stalinization. Solzhenitsyn became an overnight literary sensation in the Soviet Union, but because the novel was unprotected by copyright, his manuscript was stolen by rogue publishers in the West who paid no advances or royalties and delivered mostly inferior, poorly distributed translations. The novel, which described a single day in the life of a *Zek*—an ordinary prisoner in a Soviet labor came—failed to receive the worldwide recognition it deserved. Once Khrushchev was ousted from power in 1964, the "Khrushchev thaw" came to an end, and *One Day* was again officially taboo in the Soviet Union. Solzhenitsyn faded back into the shadows.

Understanding how the commercial publishing industry worked eluded writers like Boris Pasternak, the author of *Doctor Zhivago*, and later Solzhenitsyn. In the Soviet Union, book publishing was mostly reduced to making photocopies of a manuscript, to be passed illegally from one person to another. This so-called publishing was called *samizdat* (translation: self-publishing). As a result, Solzhenitsyn perceived publishers as essentially printers who manufactured books and made them available to the public. "In our *samizdat* culture everything was done without an exchange of money, walking a fine line between enthusiasm and the Penal Code," Solzhenitsyn would recall later in his book *Between Two Millstones*. Solzhenitsyn's lack of understanding of American publishing would play a significant role later in the sometimes-frayed communication between him and our secret group.

In the West, of course, the role of the book publisher is vastly different and is essential for the successful rollout of a book. The publisher provides an array of services that transcend printing, encompassing the entire life of the work. It selects the translator and editor, tasked with ensuring a polished literary product that potentially attracts a wide audience of readers. Once that initial work is completed, the book is generally presented to the public in a coordinated, worldwide marketing campaign through multiple media platforms and outlets. Costs associated with undertaking such a project are significant. No publisher would take on such responsibilities without copyright protection and demonstrable rights of ownership—conditions necessary to generate significant financial rewards in return for the large capital expenditures involved.

When Harrison Salisbury delivered his challenge on behalf of artists to Nikita Khrushchev, he was quickly identified by the Russian literary community as their champion.

But it took several years before the Soviet artists began to voice their pent-up frustrations and exert pressure on their repressive government. Eventually, a series of communications ensued between these dissident writers and one of Harrison's good friends, Olga Andreyev Carlisle.

Olga Carlisle was a French-born American journalist, writer and painter with strong Russian roots: The name Andreyev was well known and admired in Russian literary circles. Olga's grandfather, Leonid Andreyev, had been a major Russian writer—considered the father of Expressionism in Russian literature—and a close friend of Maxim Gorky and Leo Tolstoy. Olga's father, Vadim Andreyev, Leonid's eldest son, was also a highly regarded poet and novelist who fled the Soviet Union in the bloody aftermath of the October Bolshevik Revolution in 1917. While Olga grew up in Paris, she was a Russian beauty of shrewd intellect, reared in the world of her former country's culture and literature. And now there were whispers about a secret plan to publish in the West Solzhenitsyn's important new work, *The First Circle,* a largely autobiographical novel depicting the lives of concentration camp inmates in a research facility outside Moscow.

In the spring of 1967, Olga went to Moscow for several days to gather material for a book on contemporary Soviet poetry. Visiting with family and friends, she was invited to a small party where she had her first introduction to Solzhenitsyn. They shared a close friend; he knew Olga's parents. After they met again at another social gathering, Solzhenitsyn offered to walk Olga back to her hotel, and on the way he sprang a stunning request: "I want you to see to the publication of *The First Circle* in the West. "

Recalling the incident in her book, *Solzhenitsyn and the Secret Circle*—a detailed account of the work of our secret group in the West—Olga said she "felt limp" as Solzhenitsyn implored her to arrange for the translation and publication of the novel so that it drew as much worldwide attention as possible. It was clear that *The First Circle* would not be published in the Soviet Union. After the tumult caused by the publication of *One Day in the Life of Ivan Denisovich*, Solzhenitsyn's attempts to publish further works there were met with suspicion and bureaucratic resistance. The manuscript for *The First Circle*—even with the excision of ten chapters to make it more palatable to the censors—was denied publication.

Out of options in his home country, Solzhenitsyn had converted the shortened manuscript of *The First Circle* to microfilm and arranged to have the book smuggled to West Germany. But publishing abroad would still be an extremely dangerous undertaking. To coordinate the translation, publishing and distribution of a book of this magnitude would be daunting. It would have to be done in absolute secrecy; its origins could not be traced back to the author. Solzhenitsyn was being increasingly harassed by the KGB, who had seized many of his papers. Any misstep could result in the disappearance or death of the most celebrated Russian writer since Tolstoy.

Olga Carlisle understood the risks. But she also understood that this was a "big book," as Solzhenitsyn had told her. His was one voice that had a chance of breaking the silence surrounding Russia's repression and telling the true story of its people.

It was an offer she couldn't refuse.

Shortly after Olga returned to the United States with three canisters of microfilm, she sat down with her husband, Henry, to hatch an audacious plan. They considered having the manuscript translated and then turning it over to a publisher without any claims of authorization or participation by Olga as the intermediary. The publisher could decide what to do with it, thereby providing some security against disclosure of Solzhenitsyn's or Olga's involvement. But Henry, a writer and editor who had spent several years working for New York book publishers, believed that the better course was to secretly work with a major publisher to promote the book and guide its release worldwide; they were hoping that such fame would help protect Solzhenitsyn from Soviet persecution. The Carlisles agreed that "big books" were largely handled by major publishing houses who were willing to bet their considerable resources on manuscripts that had the potential to become international best sellers. But to enlist such a publisher, they would need help.

Olga and Henry's first step was to approach two close friends who lived near their Connecticut home, who also happened to be close friends of each other. The first was Harrison Salisbury, mentioned at the beginning of this chapter. Harrison, who had become one of my clients, had just finished producing his acclaimed history of the siege of Leningrad, *The 900 Days*. Tall and lean, Harrison moved with ease and purpose. He looked more like an English lit professor than the intrepid global reporter he actually was. The Carlisles knew Salisbury had experience in the publishing industry as well as broad knowledge of the complex political landscape in the Soviet Union.

The second person was Thomas P. Whitney, a former attaché of the U.S. government, who had been correspondent for the Associated Press, then served as bureau chief in Moscow during the same period that Harrison was stationed there for the *Times*. Tom, too, had stood in the Iowa cornfield next to Khrushchev. He was a brilliant intellect and an accomplished Russian translator whose English translation of *One Day* was widely considered to be the most accurate one. Harrison told me that Tom had actually taught himself Russian, locking himself in a room for two weeks and emerging with a working knowledge of the language.

Since Harrison and his wife were away, Olga and Henry first described the project to Tom, who enthusiastically joined up. Then the three of them approached another friend and neighbor, Cass Canfield Sr., who had been president and chairman of Harper & Row (previously Harper & Brothers) and was then the house senior editor. Canfield was a titan of the publishing industry, known for his star-studded stable of authors, from President John F. Kennedy to Leon Trotsky. Canfield had many questions but was clearly intrigued by the challenge of publishing a work of such magnitude. Still, secrecy and the safety of Solzhenitsyn were paramount; he was instructed not to mention the project to anyone, except to get an independent assessment of *The First Circle* from another of Canfield's star clients—Harrison Salisbury.

When Tom and the Carlisles met with Harrison, he was immediately on board. He agreed to read the manuscript, relay his opinion to Cass Canfield and help in any other way he could. He had one other suggestion: The project team needed a lawyer to act on their behalf, ensuring the secrecy of their identities through attorney-client privilege, providing protection for Solzhenitsyn, surmounting any legal obstacles to publication and providing professional advice about how to manage substantial revenues that might flow from the book.

"I can't recommend anybody more qualified than my lawyer, Tony Curto," Harrison told the Carlisles. I also was Tom Whitney's lawyer. Tom agreed: I was the right choice.

"You'll see, Tony will prove a great boost to your project," Harrison told Olga, as she recounted in her book. "Don't let yourself be thrown off by his all-American exterior. You will find it useful to bring some solid common sense to your Russian adventure."

That's how the project came to me. We needed to create a sound legal and financial structure for this undertaking, as well as to provide protection for Solzhenitsyn and those working on his behalf. Olga and Henry Carlisle, Harrison Salisbury, Tom Whitney and I had professional reputations to protect against any potential accusation that we had undertaken this project for personal gain, which would have been calamitous for our careers.

But first, I was faced with the immediate challenge of finding a way to secure copyright protection for *The First Circle* under the Berne Convention, to which the United States was a signatory. Ultimately, no matter how important the novel was, the task of enlisting a quality international publisher like Harper & Row would be impossible without some form of written agreement from Solzhenitsyn. Under U.S. law, a literary work without written authorization from the author would fail to secure a copyright and further raise suspicions regarding our authority to represent him. Without such copyright protection, a prestigious publisher like Harper & Row would not accept a manuscript for publication; doing so could put its reputation and large sums of money at risk.

What made things especially difficult was that Solzhenitsyn flatly refused to put anything in writing that would confirm his knowledge of, support for or involvement in publishing his works abroad. Living in a climate of fear and under constant scrutiny by the KGB, the well-known dissident was reluctant to sign any document that might implicate him in this clandestine venture. As Solzhenitsyn would recall in *Between Two Millstones,* he would not agree to any written authorization, even though he was committed to commissioning Olga—and Olga alone—to publish the book in the West. "If such a paper were to be seized at the border," he wrote, "my head would roll before any edition of *The First Circle* were to come out in print!" At the same time, being unable to produce any written agreement also would mean an end to the project as Solzhenitsyn envisioned it. If anything happened to Solzhenitsyn, there would be no proof that we had ever been working under his direct instructions and supervision.

It was not an easy assignment. And not the easiest of times for me to take it on. I was in my early thirties and had recently assumed the presidency of Tom Whitney's multi-million-dollar family business, Whitney Enterprises. I was managing hundreds of his employees while faced with solving the technical legal questions of securing a copyright for Solzhenitsyn—with no backup legal team of my own at my disposal.

As fate—or providence—would have it, two years earlier I had handled a case that would lead me to a unique solution. The case involved two brothers who were taking care of their elderly mother. They agreed that one would manage the finances while the other would provide the caregiving support. Shortly after they arrived at this understanding, their mother passed away, and the son who had assumed the financial responsibility refused to return the unspent money to his brother. He denied that their agreement was valid, claiming that under the statute of frauds section of New York State law such an agreement had to be in writing for it to be enforceable.

Representing the brother who sued the other for the unspent money, I had to confront this legal principle: Under the frauds statute at the time, any obligation that would take more than a year to perform or involve more than $1,000 would have to be in writing; any oral understanding between the parties presented in an effort to prove the validity of an agreement would not be admissible in court and therefore would fail to recover the entrusted funds. I had run straight into a legal concrete wall. How could I prove an agreement that was never put in writing and signed by the parties?

In Western jurisprudence generally, and specifically under New York State law, there is only one exception to the frauds statute when it comes to overcoming the absence of written agreements. Under trust law, if someone delivers a corpus (money or property in trust) to an individual who accepts the corpus with instructions to undertake a certain task and obligation, no agreement in writing is mandatory. Memoranda outlining the understanding, together with circumstantial facts, can prove the existence of the relationship. In the brother's case I was able to show that money was delivered to my client and that certain monies were expended on behalf of their mother. Using that argument, I won the case.

In Solzhenitsyn's case, the problem was similar. How could I enforce an oral contract necessary to support an application for copyright? I thought that by arranging for Olga to meet with Solzhenitsyn and having her write down the circumstances surrounding the delivery of the manuscript from the author, I might obtain enough legal footing to secure a U.S. copyright. So even if Russia was not a signatory to the Berne Convention, perhaps I could still get copyright protection under U.S. trust law.

In the fall of 1967, Olga Carlisle went to Moscow with a script I had drafted, which stated the understanding that Solzhenitsyn was delivering a copy of the manuscript to Olga, with instructions to arrange for the translation, publication and international distribution of the book. Solzhenitsyn recited these words to Olga, and upon returning to the United States, she prepared a document called a restatement of trust, which she swore to, authorizing her to act as trustee in managing the manuscript. Olga Carlisle evidenced the trust that was created, providing a clear and specific understanding of what Solzhenitsyn said he would do and what he had instructed Olga to do on his behalf. Since we had the manuscript (the corpus of the trust), as well as the restatement of the trust and script, I believed that we had enough authority to support a contractual relationship with Harper & Row and convince their attorney, Alan Schwartz, that it would support copyright protection under U.S. law. I cited the New York law that supported this theory. Schwartz was convinced: If the copyright and patent office of the U.S. government accepted my argument in support of the copyright application, he and his client, Harper & Row, would be satisfied.

My argument was accepted by the patent office. Schwartz was satisfied. And I was immensely gratified.

We now had a pathway to secure copyright protection without the necessity for Solzhenitsyn to deliver to us his signed written document. Solzhenitsyn would still be able to maintain his cover story, that the KGB had stolen his manuscript and published it in an attempt to blame him for writing a critical work that embarrassed the Soviet Union—a crime they would, in fact, accuse Solzhenitsyn of.

This was the beginning of the tumultuous story of how two secret manuscripts, *The First Circle,* then *The Gulag Archipelago,* came to America. The core team that assumed authority over these projects would work together almost six years. In addition to Harrison Salisbury, Tom Whitney, Olga and Henry Carlisle and me, the group comprised Cass Canfield and another top executive at Harper & Row, Win Knowlton, and Evan Thomas, a prominent journalist who had written numerous articles about the CIA. Establishing a credible foundation was essential, and the team had the unique credentials to carry it out.

After creating the legal theory to secure a copyright, I remained close to the center of this literary vortex. I was the strategist who did the legal, financial and contractual work with Harper & Row that was needed to publish the works. I hid the manuscripts in the air-conditioning ducts at my home, getting them translated by Tom (with editing help from Olga and Henry) one page at a time, with a typist in my office so that I could maintain strict security over every page of the manuscripts.

Providing accurate translations was an enormous challenge in itself, partly because of Solzhenitsyn's demanding timetable, and partly because the author had written them in *Zek*—that is, Russian laced with the slang spoken by inmates of Siberian prison camps. From the beginning, Tom Whitney worked tirelessly, often twelve hours a day, for months, to deliver complete manuscripts—every word of *The First Circle* and later the *Gulag*, which was a monumental, three-volume historical account of the Soviet prison camp system.

Solzhenitsyn had an ambitious scheme to publish a series of books in rapid succession, so he could control his storyline and the events around him. He had a multifaceted political agenda designed to expose Soviet repression and set the government back on its heels. There were considerable risks: It was the height of the Cold War, and the speed of the project was tempered by our constant concern for secrecy and the protection of Solzhenitsyn. In the Soviet Union, Solzhenitsyn was always dodging the KGB, whose agents were relentlessly scheming, searching for ways to terrorize his family and "invisible allies," damage his reputation and ensnare him in contrived plots that might put him on trial. And as the attorney involved in these projects, I, too, was under surveillance, by both the CIA and the KGB. We were all worried that Solzhenitsyn might be arrested or "disappeared" at any time.

Against this backdrop of international intrigue, we raced to publish *The First Circle* and met our target date, launching the book with Harper & Row in September 1968. While litigation was raging between other publishers over copyright claims to Solzhenitsyn's more politically benign novel, *Cancer Ward*, we had heard that he was exultant over the success of his novels in the West, and particularly grateful for the role our team played. We were already translating the *Gulag*, but it was difficult to keep up with the author's schedule, simply because of the sheer number of projects he had in the works. This job was too big for our secret group; Harrison and Tom were working without staff or compensation.

Over the next two years, the group's relationship with Solzhenitsyn was sometimes strained. With our closely watched client living in the Soviet Union, continuous communication was hard to maintain. The only reliable way to communicate with Solzhenitsyn was through intermediaries or face-to-face meetings, so Olga traveled there several times to confer with him—until she herself was denied a visa.

When Solzhenitsyn was awarded the Nobel Prize in Literature in October 1970, he decided not to travel to Stockholm to accept the prize, afraid that he would not be let back into the Soviet Union. His fears were justified. The first volume of the *Gulag* came out in Paris in late 1973, and he was expelled from his country a few months later.

Even as we celebrated Solzhenitsyn's Nobel Prize, we could see the relationship with our world-renowned client becoming increasingly complicated. Several months earlier, we were informed through an intermediary that Solzhenitsyn had decided to engage a Swiss attorney, Dr. Fritz Heeb, to act as his official legal representative in the West. Heeb was authorized to sign contracts for future books and supervise the quality of all translations of his work. While we were to retain responsibility for translation and editing of the *Gulag*, Heeb would oversee all other future publications, handling world rights, except that our team would be responsible for

English-language markets and Russian-language editions would be handled by YMCA Press, a well-known publisher in Paris.

Not surprisingly, this triangular administration of Solzhenitsyn's projects—with representatives and intermediaries working across multiple countries under difficult conditions of languages and law—did not work out well. It led to swirling rumors, confusing instructions, misunderstandings over our respective responsibilities and delays in publication that exasperated our impatient client. Ultimately, Olga decided that this shared-responsibility model could not work. She wrote to Solzhenitsyn that it was time for her and her team to step aside, relinquishing all rights and responsibilities for publishing the *Gulag*, even though Tom Whitney had already translated all three volumes of the work.

This resulted in a fiery response—literally—from Solzhenitsyn, who told Olga that she should throw the translation of the *Gulag* into Heeb's fireplace, in his presence. Well, we did not burn the translation of *Gulag*, but that gave us a window into the temperament of this former *Zek*. Instead, we set about putting Heeb in direct contact with Tom and proceeded to wind down our business with the Solzhenitsyn trust. Sadly, Solzhenitsyn would later admit that his engagement of Heeb would end in disaster, since this attorney "could not grasp the scale of my affairs and barely managed to handle anything."

I never met Solzhenitsyn, but before our tenure was over, our group would be accused by members of the press of being international book pirates, "mercenaries" playing fast and loose with his life for personal financial gain. In *Between Two Millstones*, he would identify me, based on what he had read in Olga's *Secret Circle* book, as a financial type, with little or no acquaintance with the arts. "It is not surprising," he wrote, "if Curto, who is quite indifferent to the literary and political aspects of the matter, sees only that something of material value is lying untapped, and that a hefty profit can be made from it."

In fact, I was well acquainted with the arts. I had represented many artists and was vice president of the New York State Council for the Arts. I was not "indifferent to the literary and political aspects of the matter."

Solzhenitsyn was driven by his desire to structure this deal only in artistic and geopolitical terms. But my responsibility was to protect his intellectual property and collect all the royalties, while simultaneously protecting Solzhenitsyn and his secret circle from attack and possible professional ruin. That was my mission. Solzhenitsyn's criticism was actually a supreme compliment; it meant I was doing my job.

Our small team made no "hefty profits" from the work. Over the course of six years I received about $20,000 in fees and expenses, while I made two business trips to Europe and represented Solzhenitsyn before the U.S. Tax Court to settle IRS claims against funds transferred to Switzerland. Olga and Henry together received fees and commissions averaging $11,800 a year over a period of six years. Harrison was paid nothing for his work. Tom Whitney, who translated both *The First Circle* and the *Gulag* (1,700 pages!), received no remuneration, at his own request. It was a prodigious task, but his painstaking labor, he said, was simply a contribution to Solzhenitsyn's historic undertaking.

Years later, Solzhenitsyn would note that Tom was "an honest and selfless man… not worried about the contract, or about remuneration but he was sincerely interested in furthering Russian books in America." True, Tom did not need the money—he had inherited wealth—but he also had a broad appreciation for Russian art and life. He wrote a memoir, *Russia in My Life*, which chronicled the years he spent there at the end of the Stalin regime, including his marriage to Yulya (Julie) Zapolskaya, a striking Russian folk-singer, and his struggle to bring her to the United States. Later, he endowed a center for Russian culture at his alma mater, Amherst College, to which he donated his vast library of Russian literature and hundreds of pieces of Russian art. In *Two Millstones* Solzhenitsyn would later acknowledge his frustration at trying to reconcile the "desperate rattling of the *samizdat* typewriter" with the realities of the commercial publishing world: "For me, for us, here, it was impossible to imagine how incompatible our boundless, self-sacrificing straightforwardness was with the mistrustful, corrosive, litigious approach of the West." Little did he understand that without providing for the right legal framework, his ventures could not have supported the investment of hundreds of thousands of dollars in publishing costs. There would have been no successful publication of his work, no best seller, no Nobel Prize, without the commitment of a publishing house.

Solzhenitsyn ended up receiving his prize in a 1974 ceremony, after being deported to West Germany. He lived in Switzerland before moving to the United States for seventeen years—eventually returning to Russia in 1994, after the Soviet Union had collapsed and his citizenship was restored.

Despite continuous efforts to damage his reputation, Solzhenitsyn's expulsion from the Soviet Union only bolstered his notoriety. But Solzhenitsyn's life in exile would prove trying. He was free from the strictures of a totalitarian state, but he abhorred his celebrity in the free world. He was flooded with requests, inundated with mail and under a relentless siege from the press. Followed by reporters and photographers everywhere, he lashed out one day: "You are worse than the KGB!"

In *Between Two Millstones*, Solzhenitsyn would detail his experiences and strong emotional reactions to life in the

West. While he had been sharply critical of a country whose authoritarian leaders had tried to silence his voice, he now found himself exiled in a place that supposedly embraced free speech—but was not so ready to embrace *him* when he expressed views that did not jibe with those of the cultural and political mainstream. Solzhenitsyn was constantly critiquing everything around him, and his critiques were not always well taken. In the United States, he saw a consumerist culture without roots, Godless, money driven; everything was transactional. "The West finally achieved the rights of man, and even to excess," he wrote, "but man's sense of responsibility to God and society has grown dimmer and dimmer."

Solzhenitsyn was an outsized figure who dominated the international literary scene with a messianic vision; other writers were in awe of his intellect, the speed of his writing and his prolific output. He loved humankind yet was highly critical of *people.*

From today's vantage point, much of what Solzhenitsyn criticized about the West seems to have been prophetic to me. I believe we *are* a culture in crisis. But Solzhenitsyn's views could be too singular in situations that demanded multiple views. He did not always see—or seemingly *want* to see—the role America played in bringing his work to a worldwide audience. Toward the end of our involvement, the members of our secret team remained immense admirers of Solzhenitsyn yet were saddened and confounded by the accusations and recriminations expressed against us.

Tom's inscription to me in a copy of *The Gulag Archipelago* reads as follows:

"To Tony, who saw me through this project from beginning to end, who encouraged me not to give up, who fended off

all the pirates, and who played a lead role in this whole
magnificent thing."

Ultimately, we all undertook this daunting and dangerous project, this "whole magnificent thing," because we heard that clarion call from behind the Iron Curtain, from Aleksandr Isayevich Solzhenitsyn and a whole generation of the Russian people. He was making a courageous political statement that we knew needed to be disseminated around the world.

5

Joy

*A suburban housewife-turned multimillionaire
inventor who took QVC and HSN by storm*

Joy is not only a woman's first name. It is the name of an
iconic brand.

Like Cher and Madonna, Joy is known for her roster of
unique brands, including, Miracle Mop, Rolykit, the Jewel
Kit, the Piatto Bakery Box and Huggable Hangers. With a
2015 movie, *Joy,* starring Bradley Cooper, Jennifer Lawrence
and Robert De Niro; an autobiography, *Inventing Joy,* published by Simon & Schuster; and now a musical heading
to Broadway, Joy has widened her field of influence across
the nation's consumer landscape. She has taken her rightful
place alongside the queens of branding, Oprah Winfrey and
Martha Stewart.

Behind these products and ventures is a suburban Long
Island woman named Joy Mangano—intrepid inventor,
entrepreneur and self-made multimillionaire. Those who

have met her or watched her pitch her products on TV are not surprised by her success. She speaks straight from the heart—she has the invaluable ability to understand and share the emotions of others. "When I create a product, I'm not observing consumers and trying to figure out what they need, as if they're separate from me," she wrote in her auto-biography. "I feel what *they* feel, and I need what *they* need."

Joy's cosmic achievements were among the first displayed by the generation of entrepreneurial women who burst onto the scene in the 1980s. At that time Joy was also the first woman entrepreneur I ever represented, and her story would be one of transformation, not just for her, but for me as well.

Like most men born in the 1930s, I worked for years in a male-dominated environment; women were mostly stay-at-home moms. Only three out of fifty students in my law school class were women. But the culture was changing, and when Congress passed the Equal Rights Amendment in 1972, it became clear that to be effective, men had to make significant adjustments in their behavior—both in and out of the workplace. I had a bit of a head start thanks to my mother—no shrinking violet—who taught me to listen to and be respectful of the opposite sex. Working with strong women as law partners also helped prepare me for these soci-etal changes.

But working with Joy was an altogether different experi-ence. She was not a coequal colleague; she was my client—and my boss.

Joy was a formidable force: smart, thoughtful, ambitious and doggedly determined. On top of that, she was drop-dead gorgeous. She was breaking through the glass ceiling, but not just in the corporate setting, where women were gaining legal rights against discrimination. Joy was achiev-ing great success in the entrepreneurial jungle, where there were few rules protecting women. She was leading a transformative movement—and she made me pay close attention to it.

Everyone could see that Joy was a woman in charge who knew where she was going—but it didn't start out that way. In fact, Joy's entrepreneurial inspiration came out of personal desperation. One day she suddenly found herself a young, divorced mother with three small children to support, and she realized that she needed to be "Joy the Courageous."

It's been almost thirty years since my first meeting with Joy, and I remember it well. I could sense immediately that she was a keen listener who got what you meant as soon as you spoke. I had been representing her father, Rudy Mangano, the owner of an auto body shop, in various business matters when I became aware of his new venture, manufacturing a unique self-wringing mop. Unlike traditional mops, this mop enabled users to avoid the unpleasant task of squeezing out dirty water from the mop head with their hands. Unknown to me, it was Joy who was really the brains behind this product.

The idea came to Joy one day when she was on her father's boat cleaning up a spill from one of her kids. (She knew Rudy was scrupulous about keeping a spotless deck.) She grabbed the navy mop on board and began swabbing the deck, wringing it out over the side of the boat. Ugh! There *had* to be a better way: That would become her entrepreneurial mantra.

Joy set out to create a better mop, working on hundreds of sketches before coming up with a prototype, only to be told that a company in Australia had a patent on a similar self-wringing mop. While the concept was the same, there was little comparison between the structures of the two mops. Nevertheless, rather than spend months fighting the patent issue, Joy asked her father to work out a deal with the U.S. representative of the Australian company—a man named Eddie Arnolds—that would allow her to sell her version of the mop. Under the deal Rudy negotiated, the Australian company would get a royalty for each mop sold and Joy would use Eddie's manufacturing partner, California-based West Coast Molds & Manufacturing, to make the plastic molds to fabricate the mops.

It took several months—with Joy's close supervision—to get the molds exactly right, but when the first three mops were finally delivered to her house, they worked perfectly. To celebrate, Joy took her children out for ice cream. She hadn't sold a single mop, but Joy believed no success in life is too small to celebrate. The journey to create something meaningful is too long, too hard and too unpredictable to wait until you cross the finish line. Joy was already celebrating!

But that was just the beginning of her challenges. First of all, she needed money—she had little of her own to spare. Using startup capital from her father, Joy began producing mops in the back of his auto body shop and selling them at boat shows, local flea markets and fairs for $19.99. People loved it, but it cost four times more than an ordinary mop, so she had to convince her customers that it was worth the price. Joy decided to call her new creation the Marine Mop, because that's where the idea was hatched, on a boat. While it was certainly handy on boats, Joy soon noticed that a lot of women were telling her, "Boy, I wish I had one of those in my kitchen." To which she responded, "Yeah, me too." And so, the Marine Mop was rechristened the Miracle Mop

Now Joy had to convince the buyers who controlled major distribution outlets to order her mop. She persuaded Amway to put the product in its catalog. Next, she got Kmart to agree to let her do a demonstration in one of its stores.

After the demonstration she sold hundreds of mops, but she received no word from Kmart for days—until the buyer finally called and told her that Kmart would sell the Miracle Mop in every state east of the Mississippi. On to QVC!

A few years after the launch of the Home Shopping Network (HSN), QVC had become the second network to bring products directly into the homes of millions of TV viewers. Joy did a demonstration in front of one of the company's few female buyers (it was still mostly a man's world at the time), and duly impressed, the buyer ordered five thousand mops. After a poor demonstration by a male host, however, only five hundred mops sold, and Joy was told that the unsold mops were going to be returned to her. Joy refused to give in, telling the buyer's boss that QVC was selling the mop the wrong way. The boss was skeptical, but to get this relentless woman out of his office, he agreed to put the Miracle Mop back on the air—as long as Joy, *personally*, made the sales pitch.

Thus, the single mom from Long Island with no TV experience went in front of millions and millions of viewers and just started talking, talking from the heart, telling everything she knew about the mop, as only she knew how to do. When she was done, a disbelieving QVC manager smiled broadly and informed Joy that she "broke the phones": She sold the unsold mops in twelve minutes. QVC ordered eighteen thousand mops, and then sixty thousand more. It could have been a story line right out of a movie—and years later, of course, it was.

Just as Joy was rocketing toward success, she was blindsided by another challenge that would test her entrepreneurial mettle. One day, while meeting with her father, she found out that West Coast Molds & Manufacturing was raising the price almost two dollars for each mop they produced, making it impossible for her to sell the Miracle Mop for $19.99. Joy realized that this was no less than a shakedown: West Coast had possession of her molds and was trying to steal her product. She told Rudy to get her molds back from West Coast, but Rudy said he couldn't because they owed the California company hundreds of thousands of dollars. Incredibly, her father hadn't been paying the royalties due to West Coast.

From a legal point of view, the case was a mess. Rudy's paperwork was sloppy; contracts had not been prepared and signed, delineating their ownership of the molds. Joy was caught off guard; these attacks from a potential rival could not entirely have been foreseen. The case involved multiple jurisdictions, multiple parties and multiple issues. Furthermore, it would be necessary to fight the case in California, requiring local counsel.

The logistics were daunting. And my ability to help was limited to my advising Joy and her father that we needed a patent attorney and a plan to retrieve the molds being held hostage in California. I explained what a difficult job lay ahead and gave them the name of a patent lawyer in California, John Cacagni, to get them started in the right direction.

During our strategy meeting, Rudy kept deferring to Joy when I raised questions. That surprised me. Rudy was a seasoned businessman, and to look to his daughter for direction seemed ill-advised. I saw Joy as a late-twenties-something woman with three children and a shaky home life. Where did she get the experience to even *think* that she could solve this problem? I reiterated my concerns about going forward, yet Joy insisted on fighting the case. I sent them off to meet with John with little confidence that they would prevail, given the need to resolve the matter quickly, with their limited financial resources. From years of observing our nation's civil justice system, I knew that many strong legal claims die without getting a fair hearing in court because of the amount of time and money required to pursue those claims.

Off Joy went, but this time, she was prepared. She pored over the documents and records Rudy had on file and made some surprising discoveries. For one thing, there was no documentation as to who owned the molds—no agreements or letters of understanding that Joy or anyone else owned the rights. Then, Joy made another startling discovery: Eddie had been cheating his Australian partner out of royalties for the mops, as reflected in the company's books. Armed with this knowledge, she arranged to meet with Eddie and confronted him about his fraudulent actions. Eddie was enraged, but he realized that Joy had him—there was no escape. He agreed that he would no longer receive any royalties for the mops, that Joy owed him no money and that she owned the molds.

On to California to retrieve the molds!

If you saw the movie *Joy*, or read Joy's autobiography, you would not be astounded to learn that she prevailed. As expected, West Coast Molds & Manufacturing tried to stonewall her, claiming that the molds had been stolen. "Tell you what," the CEO told her, "we'll look around and see if we can't find them." But Joy wasn't about to return to New York without the molds. She went to court to seek an emergency order, even though her lawyer told her it was an extremely long shot. Most experts believed that a judge might agree to review the issue, but no judge would likely make a decision in one day; it could take months.

When Joy went to court with her lawyer, she asked to speak directly the judge. She laid out her case, told him the whole story of how she had created the company and why she needed the molds. Without them, everything she had worked for would be lost. She talked to the judge the same way she pitched her mops, straight from the heart. When Joy finished, the judge did what was practically unprecedented: He issued an emergency order directly from the bench, requiring Joy to pay West Coast what she owed them, and

West Coast in return to deliver the molds to Joy by noon the next day—or face arrest.

What a surprise it was, not only to me but to most legal observers, when Joy came home with all issues resolved. Her mop's unique design and function ultimately supported her independent claim for patent protection under U.S. law. She was realizing her dream, selling her mops by the tens of thousands on QVC. And I learned a lesson about underestimating this woman's strength and perseverance—something I never did again in the decades we worked together.

During the years that followed, Joy and I collaborated on many matters relating to office and factory leases, banking, taxation and other corporate matters. Through her company, Ingenious Designs, she launched a succession of innovative products—simple solutions, as she put it, to common, everyday problems. There was the Rolykit, a sturdy rolling kit that could take the place of everyone's annoying "junk drawer." The Jewel Kit, a multicompartment box to solve the problem of jewelry clutter. The Piatto Bakery Box, a better way to carry pies. And the Huggable Hanger, a unique hanger that helped people unclutter their closets full of mismatched hangers and keep their clothes from constantly falling to the floor. Joy thought of herself as a consumer, and everything around her as products—including her job, relationships and family. *Everything.*

The successful handling of all these product launches ultimately brought Joy to the attention of Barry Diller, the billionaire media mogul, who already owned the Home Shopping Network. He decided that he wanted to buy Ingenious Designs—and all Joy's ingenious inventions. Later, he would acknowledge that what he wanted most was this dynamic entrepreneur, for he was sure that with her he could create a major force in the industry.

He was right.

Diller wanted Joy to be part of the executive team at HSN; support from the company's marketing people and other professionals could free her to do what she loved most, invent new things. Selling her company to HSN made a lot of sense, but it was a big move, leaving QVC for a major competitor. Joy, like a number of my other clients, would often turn to me for strategic planning advice to help her accomplish her goals. She called me her "answer man."

Every negotiation for the sale of a company starts with an asking price. Sometimes the buyer proposes a purchase price, after a review of the company's finances. But Joy wanted to make sure that the price *she* expected was put on the table first. When I asked her what she wanted she said, "Ten million." Frankly, this was substantially higher than I thought the company was worth. I asked her how she got to the figure. She answered, "That's what I will sell the company for, not one penny less." No further explanation.

I suggested that we ask for $11.5 million, which would give us some negotiating room. She would have none of it. She instructed me to go to the meeting and ask for the ten million, and not to budge. I noted how unusual that negotiating tactic was. I told her that in all my experience sellers ask for a higher price so they could offer buyers some givebacks. Usually, this approach facilitates closing a deal.

Joy wouldn't have it. She listened very carefully to my arguments. But after I was finished, she reiterated her instructions to enter negotiations with a firm asking price of ten million. Finally, we decided to back up our positions with a friendly bet: one "shiny thin dime" on whether the asking price would end up being the final selling price.

In our initial meeting, Diller's representatives were cordial. We exchanged voluminous due diligence documents relating to the financial condition of Joy's company and then answered questions that seemed to satisfy Barry's advisers.

After an awkward pause, his attorney asked what her selling price was. I knew this question was coming. With a shiny dime at risk, I pronounced that Joy would sell the company for ten million dollars—and she was firm.

There was little reaction. While I didn't detect a smirk or any rolling eyes, it was obvious that they didn't believe the company was worth that price tag. They believed there was a lot of wiggle room, and this was simply our opening gambit.

Our next meeting was a working session where in-depth questions were raised. Diller's people were sophisticated buyers, and they were looking under the hood very carefully. At the end of the session, Barry's counsel asked, "Okay, what price does Joy *really* want for the company?" I reaffirmed the ten-million-dollar figure. Frowns. It was clear they still thought the number was too high. I left the meeting uneasy and informed Joy of their resistance to her asking price. I told her that the negotiations would be difficult going forward without her being flexible. She said, "Tony, tell them that I am very firm on the price. Use whatever language you need to convince them of my position."

The next meeting was another working session to go over contracts. Draft documents were exchanged, with the space left blank for the purchase price. All the outstanding issues were resolved except for the money issue, so Diller's attorney confronted the problem head on. "Tony," he said, "let's get serious. What price will Joy take for getting what she wants?" I repeated, as forcefully as I could, Joy's insistence that she receive ten million dollars for the company. "Take it or leave it," I said. I don't recall ever using that phrase at any other time, either before or after this case.

Barry and Joy had one thing in common: Both of them knew that Ingenious Designs would not be sold for what it was actually worth, as reflected in the company's current value. They knew the price would have to be calculated based on what the company would be worth going forward, not on past performance. When I told Joy about the impasse, she had no qualms about our negotiating tactics. She trusted her instincts, and this was her price. She felt sure she would win the day.

And she did. After a couple of hours of intense back-and-forth deliberations, Barry finally agreed to purchase Ingenious Designs for ten million dollars. This was probably the most unusual negotiation in my over six decades of buying and selling assets. Never before, in any transaction I was involved with, either as a buyer or as a seller, did the initial asking price end up as the final sale price. And there went my shiny thin dime.

Over the years this pattern would repeat itself numerous times. This was the tactic we employed successfully when we negotiated her multiple-year contracts with QVC and HSN, as well as the contract on the sale of her movie rights, her book rights and her Broadway musical rights. Joy always had a firm view of the terms she expected. Believe in your ideas, she told people. Be certain of your position and stick to it.

As has happened with several other long-time clients, my professional relationship with Joy grew into a friendship that deepened over the decades. She continued to turn to me as her answer man, but in truth we learned from the other. We solved numerous issues and problems along the way, and no matter the difficulty, we always finally agreed on a course of action. Her awards and accolades mounted with her achievements: She was once named Long Island Entrepreneur of the Year by Ernst & Young and subsequently was included in *Fast Company's* annual listing of "The 100 Most Creative People in Business." She belongs in the top ranks of the entrepreneurs I've worked with, with a singular grace, enthusiasm for battle and ability to focus on the issues. It was an honor to work for her.

One last thing: I can't conclude my recollections of this extraordinary woman without commenting on her success in life overall, not just in her business career. Throughout the years, Joy Mangano has been adept at keeping her dreams and goals intertwined with those of her family and friends. When she needed to hire new employees for her growing company, she even managed to include her ex-husband—as well as both her divorced parents! She was a loving and effective parent to three outstanding children, who are now adults. They all have distinguished careers, balancing their personal and business lives with the same expertise they witnessed in their mother. In her autobiography, Joy ascribes this success to her philosophy of always looking for the best in people, instead of the worst—and that is what "allowed me to keep my little gang together for a long, long time."

6

Father Tom

The ("not Catholic enough") priest who created half of the "God Squad" and revolutionized Catholic TV

t is widely known that Father Tom Hartman had at least ten thousand "very close friends" during his lifetime.

I was lucky enough to be one of them. People often use the word "extraordinary" to describe someone like Monsignor Thomas J. Hartman. But Father Tom really *was* the most extraordinary person I've ever met. In many respects he was like Clark Kent, an anonymous Superman—except his superpower was love. I've never experienced such absolute goodness and love in any human being. And yet, you would never have known that Tom was a Roman Catholic priest upon meeting him; you just knew he was something special.

Tom Hartman was, in fact, as good-looking as Clark Kent. He stood six foot three, with a full head of sandy blonde hair. His handshake was both firm and soft. He had a gentle way of moving; he understood how to be warm and embracing, while always respectful of your personal space. Both men and women were immediately attracted to—and often confounded by—the kind of love they received from this man. Men weren't accustomed to receiving it from other men, and women were often confused by Tom's expressions of love and tenderness; they were unsure how to love him back. Few people are capable of loving in different ways, and although it wasn't easy for Tom to navigate through this thicket of emotions, he did so, gently, thoughtfully, while continuing to reinforce his values.

Father Tom Hartman was best known as the Catholic half of "The God Squad," a widely popular television show which he co-hosted with Rabbi Marc Gellman. On TV, as well as in radio appearances and in their weekly print column, the dynamic duo practiced their trademark repartee, a winning format of good-natured wisecracks mixed with serious questions about faith and belief. Rabbi Gellman was a biblical scholar of considerable renown. Tom, too, was an academic, but his defining achievement was the ability to give people a sense of comfort they rarely experienced elsewhere. I often referred to Rabbi Gellman as the "pure brains" of the team, while Father Tom was "pure love." Together, the two of them represented the ideal human being; that's why they touched so many people and were such a powerful influence during the time they had together.

Tom Hartman grew up in East Williston, Long Island, and was ordained a Roman Catholic priest in 1971. Eight years later he received his Doctor of Ministry degree from the Jesuit School of Theology at Berkeley, where he distinguished himself as a theological scholar. Tom unquestionably had the educational credentials to aspire to higher positions in the Catholic Church, so I asked him once why he didn't seem to have much interest in moving up in the hierarchy. Wouldn't he like to become a cardinal?

"Tony," he said, "I'm not Catholic enough."

One of Father Tom's initial assignments was as a parish priest at St. Vincent de Paul in Elmont, New York, a community near the Belmont Racetrack with a large Latino population that took care of the horses. He knew he was in the right place. He believed his calling was to become a parish priest in a modest middle-class community; he wanted to be close to ordinary people. It didn't take Father Tom long to distinguish himself as a loving person who just happened to be a priest.

I met Tom in 1984, as my first marriage was failing. I decided to seek counsel from three respected sources: a woman psychologist, my mother and a priest—Father Tom. Tom was introduced to me by Sandy Chapin, the wife of Harry Chapin, the folksinger and songwriter. Harry was one of my clients, but more than that, he and Sandy were my close friends, and I trusted their judgment. So, I called up Father Tom and we arranged to have lunch at La Marmite, a local French restaurant.

I soon learned that Tom's church was wherever he was: no formal office or rectory, just wherever you felt comfortable. Tom himself always seemed right at home wherever he was. I will never forget how much I trusted him as I poured out my feelings to him, and I will forever value the comfort and guidance he gave in helping me face the painful end of a twenty-year marriage. From that day on, until Tom was struck with Parkinson's roughly twenty years later, we spoke almost every day.

Father Tom was always a devoted follower of his faith. But he also managed to remain an independent thinker who delivered the teachings of the church in surprising ways. He had the uncanny ability to mix a strong entrepreneurial spirit with the Holy Spirit.

As Father Tom's ministry matured, he had the opportunity to work with a friend and fellow priest, Father Bill Ayers. Tom had first met Father Ayers when both were assigned to serve at St. James Church in Seaford, on the south shore of Long Island. Ayers, who always loved radio broadcasting, was hosting a weekly radio show called "Religion and Rock," aimed at bringing the spiritual aspect of music to a younger audience. Ayers handed over the hosting reins to Tom, who proved to be a natural, weaving his spiritual message with the music of the Beatles, Jefferson Airplane and the Who.

A few years later, Tom's friendship with Father Ayers would lead to another opportunity that would change not only Tom's life, but the place of the Catholic Church in the nation's media landscape. In the late 1970s, Ayers was in line to take over as director of Telecare, the cable TV station run by the Diocese of Rockville Centre. Charles Dolan, the founder and owner of Cablevision, had generously made the channel available for daily Catholic programming to 70,000 homes on Long Island. However, before Bill Ayers had assumed the management of Telecare, he decided to leave the priesthood altogether and focus full-time on charitable work—the creation of an organization to defeat world hunger with Harry Chapin. Bill told the diocese that he had someone in mind as his replacement: Tom Hartman.

Early on in Tom's career, when Bishop Fulton Sheen became ill, he asked Tom to visit him and talk about a new approach to promoting Catholicism. The elderly bishop had become a legend for his pioneering radio and television programs, starting with "The Catholic Hour" on NBC radio in 1930, then moving to TV with "Life Is Worth Living" and later "The Fulton Sheen Program." The bishop told Tom at this bedside meeting that the best way to evangelize Catholicism was through TV, and he believed that Tom had the faith and the personality to carry out this work. Thus, the baton was passed to Father Tom, who accepted the sacred responsibility of advancing the teachings of Christ through the power of TV.

But he would do it *his* way.

Tom knew that people who entered a Catholic church were likely to be a Catholic, but people who watched TV could be of any faith—Hindu, Lutheran, Muslim or Jew. He decided to shape Telecare's programming to take advantage of this potentially broad, diverse audience, bringing in rabbis, pastors, imams, people of faith from every racial and ethnic background, each with his or her own perspective. Instead of separating religious communities and giving viewers reasons to do so, he chose to initiate programs that minimized the differences among people and their faiths. He reinforced *commonality*.

At the center of Tom's ministry was his endless capacity for supporting people in distress. Even after he became a radio and TV personality, recognized wherever he went, he found time to provide comfort to those in need, not only in his own congregation, but across the New York area. Tom served as chaplain to the Nassau County Police Department for eighteen years. He loved sports, once telling Dan Rather in a TV interview that when he was nine years old, he decided he wanted to be either a professional baseball player or a priest. But when he hit only .250 in his young baseball career, he said to himself, "Hmmm, I better become a priest."

Father Tom did become a pretty fair tennis player and golfer, and he served as chaplain to the New York Jets—and anyone else who felt the need to be close to God. Tom often went without sleep for days at a time, meeting the demands of his ministry. I came to discover that Tom Hartman and Harry Chapin shared this quality: They could never say no to anyone.

I, too, was the recipient of Father Tom's boundless ministry. When I was in the hospital for a hernia operation, Tom came to visit me. Often, he made rounds to local hospitals to visit with people he knew, as well as those he didn't know but had been asked to visit. This was part of his regular routine; there were always people who needed caring. When Tom visited me during the day, he would usually bring me a thick milkshake. Other times, he could only find time to visit me late at night, when I was asleep. I would wake up to find a candy bar next to the bed—his way of saying that he was there but didn't want to bother me.

Is there a greater expression of love, to have someone think of you, take the time to visit you, when you're in pain and alone in a place like a hospital? Especially if that person was Tom, someone you admired, someone you knew had a special spiritual connection with the divine? It was such an honor, something that could only be experienced as a pure gift.

Over thirty years I would see the bestowal of that gift repeated over and over with other people. My wife, Linda, and I often included Tom in our family's plans, and it was not unusual for us to meet at a restaurant. As Father Tom entered, people would immediately come up to him, get in line and wait their turn to speak.

I remember one occasion in particular—my birthday—when I was hosting a party for group of friends at Rothmann's Steak House in East Norwich, Long Island. As soon as I came through the door with Tom, people rushed to see him. I went to our table and waited; it was forty-five minutes before he got there. Everyone in the restaurant appeared to have something to say to him or wanted to thank him for some act of kindness. He had amazing patience. And being around Tom, *you* had to be patient, too, because he was not going to be rushed. He would not allow a person to feel that they were taking him away from other commitments, and when that person was finished talking, they were inevitably followed by someone else who felt equally compelled to speak with him. Whether we were in New York, the Caribbean, Scotland or Florida, the scene was the same. You could see that people were visibly moved by their brief moments with Father Tom; he connected with each one of them.

At Telecare, Tom's widening TV audience got to see his unusual ability to engage people with diverse opinions in challenging conversations. One of his programs, "Father Tom and Friends," offered a no-holds-barred secular view of the business world. In each show a set of moral choices was presented for discussion to a panel of participants composed of a newspaper columnist, Ed Lowe; a black business executive from Avon, Fitzroy Hilaire, and me. (I served on the Telecare board and was also Tom's personal and family lawyer.) Over a ten-year period, we recorded hundreds of shows that played and replayed thousands of times.

Tom's most successful show was the "The God Squad." Like many breakthrough ideas, the show was the product of serendipity. One day in 1987, Cablevision's News 12 Long Island channel enlisted Tom to do short segment on Easter and Passover. When the producers wanted a rabbi to join him, he recommended Marc Gellman, whom he knew only by reputation. Rabbi Gellman was the leader of Temple Beth Torah, a big synagogue in Melville, Long Island, and a religious scholar—the youngest rabbi ever to be ordained by Hebrew Union College. That day's on-air chat led to a lengthy follow-up conversation during which Gellman told Tom that he was about to accept a job offer at a synagogue in Florida. "You're not going to Florida," Tom told him. "I had a dream last night, and God said in the dream, 'Tell the guy you're with that I'm not through with him there, where he is.'"

And so "The God Squad" was born. The working priest and the working rabbi were an odd religious couple, Tom playing the straight man to Gellman's comedic jabs. It was hard to explain their special chemistry, even for them. Years later, Rabbi Gellman would recall that Father Tom was "very, very attractive…and I was funny. Tommy could not tell a joke and I looked as if I had slept under a bridge in my suit. That was just the way it was. We were two different types, but in a certain way we were like a duet in which the music melded when were together."

The priest and the rabbi agreed that the moral tenets guiding the world's great religions are similar: They all teach love, compassion, hope, tolerance and healing. Their message is simple: If people could get over the differences between religions, they could create a common ground based on an exploration of issues ranging from the nature of God to the obligations of those who were followers of a particular faith. Tom Hartman and Marc Gellman would remain steadfast in spreading this message, wherever they appeared. They would also become best friends.

Following a decade at Cablevision, "The God Squad" moved to Telecare. After the show was syndicated, it reached fifteen million homes a week at its peak. Hartman and Gellman became household names, leading to a nationally syndicated newspaper column and regular TV and radio appearances, including nationwide shows such as ABC-TV's "Good Morning America." They were even regular guests on "Imus in the Morning," the hugely popular radio show produced by shock-jock Don Imus, which reached a daily audience of seven million people. (Tom officiated at Imus's wedding.) It was during one of those appearances that Imus coined the phrase " Father What-a-Waste," referring to Tom's good looks.

Together, Father Tom and Rabbi Gelman wrote four books, including *Religion for Dummies*. They made as many as one hundred fifty speeches a year and won four Emmy Awards for their TV work. The twosome received a Peabody Award for an HBO special based on their children's book of the same name, "How Do You Spell God?", in which they were immortalized as animated figures. Clearly, something new was emerging. While the God Squad had no agent or 800 number, its message of commonality and unity was gaining ground in mainstream America.

Pioneers like Tom Hartman invariably needed some financial backing to help build their dreams. In Tom's case, it meant a cadre of prominent men and women who supported his ministry. One of them was Michael Pascucci, an accomplished local entrepreneur who achieved phenomenal success at a young age, founding several successful ventures. He was also a devout Christian who put God first. Michael was there when Tom took the reins at Telecare and served as a long-time board member, always backing Tom financially.

One day, I asked Michael how his relationship with Tom and Telecare came about. Early on, Tom had asked Michael to accompany him to New York City to meet with a young couple. They were early for the appointment, so they decided to stop at a cafeteria for a quick bite. When they left Michael thought Tom was behind him, but he wasn't. He was still inside, looking after a homeless man and making sure that he got enough to eat. When he exited with his new congregant, Tom motioned to Michael to pay the bill. In that instant, Michael told me, he knew his role. Tom was the messenger; he was the exchequer. They would play these roles for the rest of their lives together.

Tom's legendary commitment to providing care and comfort to people in distress would sometimes result in unexpected stories, both funny and poignant. Rabbi Gellman's favorite story, which he liked to retell, involved a night that he and Tom went out for pizza and beer, but first stopped off at a hospital because Tom said he wanted to minister to a woman dying of cancer. The woman in Room 402 was alone, staring blankly out the window. Father Tom sat down on a chair next to the woman and gently took her hands. Then, Rabbi Gellman recalled, Tom said to her, "Dear, you are going to die, but you have nothing to fear because God is going to hold your soul in his hands like a little bird."

Gellman, who was standing by the door, was stunned; he had never seen anyone talk with such honesty to a dying person. Tom asked the woman whether she was still afraid, and she answered, "Yes, Father, I am still afraid." Calmly, Tom continued to try to assuage the woman's fears, but when he asked her again if she was afraid, she repeated, quite agitated, that she was.

"Why are you still afraid?" "Tom asked.

"Because," she said, sobbing, "I just came here for a hernia operation."

With that, Father Tom grabbed Rabbi Gellman and the two made a hasty retreat, outracing the security guards. Later, Gellman recalled, a still perplexed Father Tom mused, "Maybe the dying woman was in Room 502."

On another occasion, Father Tom was delivering a graveside service at a local cemetery. It was an ugly day—dark, rainy, windy, muddy. The lectern was made of Styrofoam. Suddenly, a gust of wind blew over the lectern, and as Tom lunged to save it, he slipped and fell into the grave. Not the least bit rattled, he climbed out of the hole, covered from head to toe in mud. He broke into a big smile. And he finished the service.

Sometimes Tom's caring ministry raised the eyebrows of the church hierarchy. In one instance he became spiritual advisor to a fellow named George Anderson. Psychic

George, as he was known, would bring together small groups who had recently lost loved ones and act as a medium. Tom saw that many people were comforted by George's work and wanted to help. When the bishop became aware of Tom's work, however, he was told to end his involvement. The bishop apparently felt Tom already had enough on his plate.

One day in the fall of 1986, I asked Tom if he'd like to go to Freemantle, Australia, to see the America's Cup yacht races. It promised to be an exciting event, with the fiercely competitive Dennis Conner attempting to win back the cup he lost in the 1983 Newport regatta. Without hesitation, Tom said, "Count me in." He was always up for new adventures. During that three weeks, we were together all the time. We shared a room in the Fremantle Inn, and one night when I awoke to use the bathroom and returned to the bedroom, I saw I gigantic hump in the middle of Tom's bed. It looked like an elephant under the blanket. I peeked under the covers to discover Tom sitting cross-legged with the lamp from the end table, writing postcards to people back home. Sweat was pouring down his face. He said that he wanted people to know that he was still thinking of them even though he was far away. I thought how blessed I was, that I had a friend who was so considerate that he got under the covers on a scorching summer night so I wouldn't be disturbed by the light of his lamp.

I was astounded to witness how Father Tom treated *everyone* with the same courtesy and respect. From time to time, I would invite friends—highly successful people who maintained that they were agnostic, sometimes atheist, in their beliefs—to join Tom and me for dinner. They would come armed, prepared to joust with Tom. He would have none of it. He never spoke in dogmatic terms, nor would he fall into any confrontational communication trap. His behavior was his sermon; his conduct was his message. It was a sight to behold! The way these doubters received him, it was as if some fairy had sprinkled dust over them.

One friend, a Jewish divorce lawyer, said that he had never experienced such warmth and grace, and that if he had met Father Tom earlier, he would have become a Catholic. Another good friend was an agnostic who struggled with the thorny question: How could God inflict so much pain on the world? He just couldn't believe the world was God's creation. But he, too, was stymied by Father Tom. It was as if the tenets of a religion could be displaced by the sheer embodiment of goodness.

I never knew where Father Tom's loving strength and wisdom came from, but I saw it work over and over, healing people with all kinds of troubles. I wondered: Did he bring this quality to the church or did the church release this remarkable personality? The people who knew him best, his four siblings, called him a saint. I think this goodness was just who Tom was, and it was within him all his life.

In 2003 Father Tom broke the news of his Parkinson's diagnosis in his weekly newspaper column. He had kept it a secret for several years, but it was no longer possible to hide the disease. Tom eventually stepped down as head of Telecare and ended his role on "The God Squad," as well as the syndicated column. But Father Tom's ministry did not stop. He started the Thomas Hartman center for Parkinson's Research at Stony Brook University, often working with high-profile Parkinson's patients like the actor Michael J. Fox. (Years earlier, after his brother, Gerry, died of AIDS, he had raised millions of dollars for AIDS research and helped establish a hospice for AIDS sufferers in Uniondale, Long Island.)

As his disease advanced, Father Tom moved into a nursing home, where he was visited by a stream of family and friends over the course of ten years. At the end, the man whose words had given comfort to thousands wasn't able to communicate in words, but he could squeeze your arm as a response in conversation.

Monsignor Thomas Hartman died on February 16, 2016, at only 69. His physical presence was gone, but he left an indelible legacy of love, inclusiveness and goodness, promoted through television, which he believed was increasingly vital to ensuring the relevance of the church. Today, Telecare has been rebranded the Catholic Faith Network, and now with streaming services, CFN potentially can reach billions of viewers worldwide.

Rabbi Marc Gellman, who retired as the head of his synagogue, still writes "The God Squad" column, which is distributed nationally. Even the name has become an iconic piece of our culture. Shortly after Tom's death, Rabbi Gellman recalled that after many lectures and speeches they gave, people would come up to them, often holding hands, and say, "Hey, we're a God Squad, too. She's Jewish and I'm Catholic. And we're best friends."

It's impossible to say what the future might have been like, but there's one thing I'm sure of: If Father Tom had had a normal lease on life, his ministry with Rabbi Gellman could well have had a major impact in reshaping the course of our country. They were way ahead of their time; what they did was so extraordinary that no one had done it before, and no one has done it since. Their message of commonality remains even more important today, when people are so angry that they turn their backs on those they disagree with. This rare pair—a priest and a rabbi who were best friends—was simply a work of amazing grace.

7

Christian Lopez / Derek Jeter

*A historic hit, a lucky catch and a courageous decision
that stunned America*

In his Pulitzer Prize–winning 1957 book, *Profiles in Courage*, John F. Kennedy depicted acts of bravery and integrity by eight major figures in American history, all U.S. Senators, who suffered significant losses when they bucked their political parties and their constituencies and stood up for moral principles.

Kennedy, who had been interested in acts of political courage since his college days at Harvard, found an unexpected opportunity to explore the topic when he took a leave of absence from the Senate to recover from back surgery. The resulting collection of stories described the adversity these senators faced when they followed their consciences, despite the enormous pressure to appease their constituencies and powerful interest groups.

While most of us are not politicians, we are all confronted with situations in which we must decide whether to support our moral principles despite knowing the losses we would sustain by honoring them. Over the course of my career, two particular instances stand out—separated by just a few days—where I observed individuals who maintained great character and fortitude under difficult circumstances.

The first instance was on July 9, 2011, a lazy Saturday afternoon of baseball in the New York City, when I—along with the rest of America—learned the story of Christian Lopez, a quiet twenty-three-year-old cellphone salesman from the tiny upstate town of Highland Mills. Christian was at Yankee Stadium, watching the New York Yankees play the Tampa Bay Rays with his father, Raul "Chico" Lopez. In the third inning, Yankee shortstop Derek Jeter came to bat. He needed one more hit to qualify him for entrance into the exclusive 3000-hit club in professional baseball. Only twenty-three players in the history of the game had accomplished this goal, so Derek's achievement would guarantee his place in the pantheon of stars who played the game. The count was two and two when David Price, the pitcher for Tampa Bay, wound up and delivered a fast ball. Jeter smashed it for a home run—one of five hits he had that day.

Sitting in the leftfield stands, Christian Lopez, a six-foot-plus man with boyish looks and quick hands, stretched forward and caught Derek's home run ball. He cradled it against his chest and bent forward on the barrier to protect it from the lusting fans around him. His father jumped on top of Christian to ensure the safety of his son's catch and whispered, "You can pay off your student loans now and have plenty of money left over." Christian responded: "This is Derek Jeter's ball, and I'm going to give it back to him."

Instantly, Christian had made a decision: Against his own financial self-interest, he was going to honor his moral code and Derek Jeter's historic event. The ushers at the ballpark quickly arranged for him and his father to meet Jeter and guided them into the bowels of Yankee Stadium. Everyone surrounding Christian was wondering what he would say under the bright lights of recorded history. His words were simple: "Mr. Jeter, this is your ball and I would like you to have it."

Everyone was shocked. By several estimates, the ball was worth upward of a quarter of a million dollars, and it would be a coveted piece of baseball memorabilia that undoubtedly would become more valuable as time passed. Sports writers, radio commentators, financial analysts, baseball fans and practically everyone else had an opinion about what Christian might have done with the ball: kept it, sold it, donated it to charity, given it to his dad, who almost caught the ball himself. (The ball "landed right in my hand," Raul Lopez told the *New York Post*, "and then it bounced out.") Raul admitted that while he was proud of his son, "I think I would have handled it differently if I had held onto the ball."

Christian probably could have demanded a lot from the Yankees, who, after all, were paying Jeter fifteen million a year at the time. But that's not what was on Christian's mind. "The Yankees didn't pressure me to give the ball back to Jeter. I just wanted to give it back for everything that the guy has done for us."

The Yankees did give Lopez luxury box tickets for the rest of the season; and the Yankee captain gave him three signed baseballs, three signed bats and three signed jerseys. He also received a Yankees World Series ring for 2009 (Jeter's last World Series), courtesy of Mitchell Modell, CEO of Modell's Sporting Goods, a sponsor of the team. Modell and Brandon Steiner, CEO of Steiner Sports, each guaranteed Lopez at least $25,000 toward his outstanding student loans to St. Lawrence University, which reportedly totaled around $150,000. And Topps Baseball Cards gave Christian his own card for 2011. Christian was an avid collector as a kid, claiming a stash of several thousand cards. His most prized: a card with Babe Ruth and one of the Yankees' owners when Ruth came over from the Boston Red Sox in 1920.

Still, I believe very few people appreciated Christian's act that day—and fewer would have replicated it. This became strikingly evident less than four years later. On June 21, 2015, a year after Jeter retired, his superstar teammate, Alex Rodriguez, got his three-thousandth hit at Yankee Stadium—also a home run. The ball was caught by a fan named Zack Hample. Did he return it to A-Rod? Nope. He refused, saying that he would consider working with Rodriguez and the Yankees in a joint venture to raise money for charity. In his postgame interview, Rodriguez said he wished "Jeter's guy" had caught the ball.

As I watched this story unfold, I was moved by Christian's extraordinary behavior. It was a simple, noble act. He spoke his mind, no grandiose explanation. Christian never wavered in his decision to return Derek Jeter's ball. "I would have done it over again a hundred times," he said. "I think I did the right thing." I began to think about people who did things against their self-interest, adhering to some internal moral compass, and I decided to reach out to Christian.

I wrote a letter to him and his parents, expressing my high regard for his acts and enclosing a small check to help him make a dent in his student loans. I explained that my reasons for writing the letter were both to recognize the act as being heroic and to comfort his parents for the decision that Christian had made. In about three weeks' time, I got a written response, thanking me for the note and the check. Shortly thereafter, I got a call from Christian's father, explaining that his son had been offered a job at Modell's Sporting

Goods because Christian was now elevated to the station of "sports celebrity." Raul Lopez wanted me to review the contract, so I did, *pro bono.*

Then, when Topps approached Christian to create his own card, the family asked me to review his contract with the company. Several months later, the family's accountant called and said he was preparing Christian's tax return and was concerned that Christian would have to show the income of $250,000—the value of the ball—and then file a gift tax return of an equal amount. (Derek Jeter was not a charitable organization so the gift would not be tax deductible.)

After some thought, I advised the accountant of a legal theory that I thought could defeat any claim of taxation on the event: essentially, that Christian simply found the ball and was returning it to Derek. I assured the family that I would defend the case up to the U.S. Tax Court *pro bono,* but the IRS never challenged the issue.

At the end of the year *The New York Times* identified various athletes and events the editors felt were noteworthy and reflected the best qualities of sportsmanship and the world of sports. Christian Lopez's selfless act was prominently mentioned in a short article.

Just a few days after the story of Derek Jeter's three-thousandth hit, I saw an article on the front page of *The Wall Street Journal* about an American soldier, Staff Sergeant Leroy Petry, an Army Ranger who was assigned to D Company, 2nd Battalion, 75th Ranger Regiment. Petry was being presented with the Medal of Honor, the nation's most prestigious military award, by President Barack Obama, for unselfishly risking his life to save his fellow Rangers—despite being under enemy fire and grievously injured.

At first glance, the stories of Christian Lopez, a Yankees fan from Highland Mills, New York, and Leroy Petry, an Army Ranger from Santa Fe, New Mexico, might have appeared worlds apart. But I was struck by the similarity of the moral fiber displayed by each of these two men; they could have traded places, and either would have acted the same way as the other.

Leroy Petry's story begins on May 26, 2008, in Afghanistan's Paktia Province, along the Pakistani border. He and his team assaulted a walled compound, looking for a top al-Qaeda leader thought to be there. It was a risky mission, in broad daylight. Petry was supposed to be serving in an oversight role, but when he realized that one of the assault squads needed some assistance clearing their assigned building, he moved forward to an outer courtyard, taking a fellow Ranger, Pfc. Lucas Robinson, with him. Three Taliban fighters then opened fire with AK-47s, shooting Petry in both legs and hitting Robinson in the side. Although severely wounded, Petry tried to help Robinson to safety by a chicken coop, as the insurgents continued firing.

Petry threw a grenade toward the enemy position, momentarily silencing their fire. But a Taliban fighter responded with another grenade that landed about ten meters from Petry, Robinson and another Ranger, knocking them to the ground, further wounding Robinson and wounding the other soldier. Then, a third grenade. This one landed just a few feet away from the Rangers.

"Every human impulse would tell someone to turn away," noted President Obama during the Medal of Honor ceremony for Petry at the White House. "Every soldier is trained to seek cover. That's what Sergeant Leroy Petry could have done. Instead, this wounded Ranger, this twenty-eight-year-old man with his whole life ahead of him, this husband and father of four, did something extraordinary. He lunged forward, toward the live grenade. He cocked his arm to throw it back."

As Petry opened his hand to release the grenade, it exploded. He saved all three of their lives, but not his right hand, which he saw was completely blown off at the wrist. "It was vivid," he later recalled, "where I could see the black marks where the burn marks were. And a little bit of the dirt and the smell of explosives." He sat up and put a tourniquet on his arm to prevent further blood loss. Then he did what senior officers are trained to do: Focus on the soldiers around him. "The younger guys next to me were kind of in shock and awe," he recalled. The important thing was to maintain control and awareness, "trying to maintain calm— so they stay calm."

With reinforcements, the Rangers were able to suppress the insurgents and secure the compound, although another soldier was wounded and later died. Petry spent several weeks in recovery in Germany and then Fort Hood, Texas. He was eventually fitted with an advanced prosthetic in place of his right hand, where he fastened a small plaque with the names of all the fallen Rangers from his regiment. Leroy Petry could have retired with honors. Instead, he re-enlisted in the Army, despite continuing struggles with battle wounds, and went on to work as an advocate for ill and injured Rangers and their families.

In today's transactional, material culture, when people routinely act to preserve their own self-interest, neither Leroy Petry nor Christian Lopez chose to do so, when such decisions would have been the safe, acceptable choice. What compels such courage?

While the motivation for these kinds of acts is not always easy to understand, what we know is that they reveal a moral code and individual strength, reflecting the principles upon which they act. Leroy Petry was not thinking of himself; he responded to his innate sense of a duty to protect the well-being of his Ranger brothers in harm's way. "It was almost instinct—off training," Petry recalled.

Lopez's circumstance was very different, but his decision will stand the test of history, even if not immediately seen as heroic. Then and now, Christian believes he had no choice but to honor Derek Jeter and be loyal to the Yankee tradition—and more important, to himself as a fan of the Yankee captain and his team. "I made the decision that was right for me," Christian recalled years later. "If it happened again, I'd do it the same way."

Like other Americans who have stood out as profiles in courage, these men took a great risk and paid a significant price for their courage, each losing something precious: Lopez a baseball worth a substantial fortune; Petry, his right hand—and almost his life. We all have principles with which we measure our own self-worth and integrity. In general, however, most of us recognize special kinds of behavior that are truly unique.

Coincidentally, both Petry and Jeter officially retired in 2014.

Over the course of his career, Leroy Petry was deployed eight times, to Iraq and to Afghanistan. After retirement he became a highly sought-after speaker and worked with nonprofit organizations, escorting wounded veterans back to Afghanistan for Operation Proper Exit.

Six years after stepping off the infield of Yankee Stadium for the last time, Derek Jeter was elected to the National Baseball Hall of Fame, receiving 396 of the 397 ballots cast by the Baseball Writers' Association—second only to former Yankees teammate Mariano Rivera's 100 percent vote in 2019. He was a member of five World Series championships, was named to fourteen All-Star teams, had eight 200-hit seasons, batted .300 twelve times and won five Gold Glove Awards for fielding. He was the longest-tenured Yankee captain, having held the title for twelve seasons. Jeter went on to become CEO of the Miami Marlins.

But most baseball observers agree that Derek Jeter's career was defined as much by indelible moments as by his statistics. When it mattered most, Jeter delivered. He ranks near the top of many career categories for postseason play and was named MVP for the World Series in 2000, when the Yankees beat the Mets. In his final game at Yankee Stadium, he broke a tie with a ninth inning walk-off single against the Baltimore Orioles. After being mobbed by his teammates, he walked around the infield, waving his hat to the thousands of fans who kept chanting, "*Der-ek Je-ter, Der-ek Je-ter!*" to their retiring hero.

And so it was with Christian Lopez: When it mattered most, he delivered. I would hope that as the Yankee Captain reflects back on his playing years, the day of his three-thousandth hit resonates as a glorious moment when an individual, without regard to personal gain, thought only of the significance of this event in his life and attempted in his own way to bring honor to its memory.

8

The Sting Act II

An unorthodox crew that won a world sailing championship—only after suffering bewildering losses that never actually were losses

More than forty years ago, a fat little boat sailed out of Northport Harbor and turned yacht racing on Long Island Sound upside down.

Only the elder statesmen of the racing community today can say they saw the *Sting Act II* as she swept down the Sound in the summer of 1975, collecting one win after another on the way to Block Island Race Week. And only a few can say they watched this swift boat inexplicably lose again and again during Race Week, except for one stunning race when she skimmed across a shallow ledge on the north side of Block Island while other bewildered boats tried to follow and found themselves hard aground.

But I remember well the stinging pain of losing all that week—especially since I would discover weeks later that the *Sting Act II* hadn't lost at all!

It is a story is worth retelling, partly because it shows that it's sometimes hard to recognize beauty in yacht design before a race result is posted. It also reminds us that everyone (even veteran race committees) makes mistakes; and that we need to find a way to respond to such mistakes with poise and practicality, even when they hand an unjust loss to a crew that never lost.

The success of the *Sting Act II* actually began with the failure of its predecessor, the *Sting*. In the early 1970s I met a nationally renowned sailor from a small town in southern New Jersey named Bob Seidelman. Bob was also an expert sailmaker and boat designer, and we had many interesting discussions about design and racing. We decided to form a joint venture to build a boat that could be used for cruising and racing.

Over the course of the late winter and spring of 1974, our discussions resulted in a boat that was twenty-five feet long, with an external keel and inboard rudder. We were convinced we had created a remarkable racing machine.

But even after sailing hard all summer, our results were disappointing. In thirteen races we came away with only a couple of second-place finishes and one win. The *Sting* was handsome enough, but considering the effort we'd put in, it was a pretty modest return.

Faced with the challenge of making some improvements over the winter and trying again next season, I decided instead to radically redesign the boat. I moved it into an old barn on the corner of Middleville Road and 25A in Northport, Long Island, and bought in a redesign team. And a chain saw.

At first glance, my redesign team must have seemed as unorthodox as the boat we were working on. The lineup included two Grumman engineers; a former navigator for Ted Turner, the famed media entrepreneur and captain of the twelve-meter *Courageous*, which would win the America's Cup; a physicist and champion sailor of One Design racing boats; an oyster boat captain; and an old world shipwright. We had no naval architect on the bench, nor an engineer trained in traditional yacht design.

As it turned out, this improbable crew was a perfect blend of sailing instinct and technological savvy. They knew how to go fast under sail. And they knew how to optimize the design, applying a lot of Grumman computing power. Together we set out to create a boat that would be strong and seaworthy, very fast through the water and highly advantaged under the Midget Ocean Racing Club (MORC) handicap rule. (MORC was a group of 2,100 sailors who participated in races from Canada to South America.)

The original *Sting* was twenty-five feet long, with an eleven-foot beam and a thirty-two-foot mast. Below the waterline she had a conventional inboard rudder and a 1,200-pound fin keel that drew four feet six inches. The design of the *Sting* had been brave in some respects, but timid in others. While we had followed some inspired design principles, we hadn't pushed the envelope far enough. Because of its wide beam, the *Sting* looked unconventional, especially in those days, but it was really quite ordinary. That was the problem. The design was too predictable, too cautious, too slow.

The redesigned *Sting Act II* was twenty-three feet long, cutting two feet from the stern—that's where the chain saw came in handy. We raised the mast to forty feet. There was no keel at all. We installed a centerboard but no inboard rudder; the outboard rudder was capable of being fully retracted. With her centerboard and outboard rudder fully retracted, she drew only nine inches. Think of it as a very wide, twenty-three-foot Laser sailboat.

The boat was internally ballasted with 700 pounds of lead BBs, fiberglassed into the bilge of the boat. This eliminated 500 pounds. The boat's wide beam gave us enormous form stability, which substituted for the righting ability that comes with lead in a fin keel. On deck, we gained a lot of power by raising the rig eight feet. This required us to install all new running and standing rigging and cut all new sails as well.

With all that power and reduced wetted surface, the boat flew downwind in light air. Upwind in a breeze, she heeled over until those enormous bilges hit the water, and then she locked into position and charged to windward. It was as if we were riding on a locomotive!

Our plan was to start off racing locally in and around the harbor. If we were successful, we would move on to races in western Long Island Sound and then to races on the regional level. After the first couple of races, we knew we were steering toward Block Island Race Week and our ultimate goal, the international MORC championship at the end of the year.

From the start, the *Sting Act II* was impressive. After winning some local races, we won the Winkle Cup, the Katrina Cup, the Stratford Shoal Race and then the Block Island Feeder Race. Along the way, we made some minor changes to the sails and rigging, but we didn't change much. We were thrilled with our boat speed upwind and downwind, in all conditions. We were also pleased to have won every race we entered—until Block Island.

Every two years, coinciding with the Bermuda International Invitational Race Week, the Storm Trysail Club would host Block Island Race Week, a week-long regatta comprising a series of five races. When the first starting gun went off at Block Island, we were confident. But suddenly and inexplicably, we were crushed by the competition in race after race.

The only bright spot was a race on the north side of Block Island, when the fleet sailed for the buoy that marks the end of the island's northern ledge, Buoy 1BI. In those days, yachts were not required to sail seaward of that buoy, so having sailed inside the buoy earlier and taken soundings, we peeled off from the fleet and sailed straight for the ledge. As the reef rose beneath us, we raised our centerboard and rudder more and more…until we drew only inches beneath the waterline. We held our breaths and watched shells on the bottom pass beneath us. The *Sting Act II* skimmed over the reef along the shoreline, having cut miles from the course. It was an amazing sight—though probably not so much for the crews of the boats that ran aground trying to follow us into the shoal water.

That experience was exhilarating, and thanks to that dramatic maneuver we won the race. But otherwise, Race Week was a disaster. In five days of racing we had won only that one race.

The weeks after the Block Island regatta were full of confusion and frustration. What had happened? How could we have lost to all the boats we had beaten handily in prior races? We couldn't understand how our racing fortunes had suddenly changed.

It wasn't until seven weeks later, while preparing for the international MORC championship, that I took a careful look at the Block Island results and realized that a terrible mistake had been made. The Trysail Club, which was responsible for the officiating during Block Island Race Week, had used the wrong time allowance tables for the MORC races.

In sailboat racing, each class of boats has its own handicap rule and rating, with its own time allowance chart. The

International Offshore Racing club (IOR) has a specific time allowance chart, as do MORC and the Performance Handicap Racing Fleet (PHRF). The Trysail Club had mistakenly calculated our race results using the IOR time allowance tables instead of the MORC tables, thus distorting the results. When I recalculated the results using the proper MORC allowance time chart, the *Sting Act II* won all its races.

Five first-place finishes!

With more than forty boats in our division and nearly three hundred boats in the regatta, the *Sting Act II* should have been named the winner in its class and been honored with the award for the best boat of the week. John Stork, a flag officer of the Trysail Club and a well-respected member of the Northport Yacht Club, reviewed the matter with me. John, one of the best offshore sailors our harbor had ever produced, agreed with my findings. But he explained that nothing could be done about changing the results. The period for protest had long since expired.

In the nation's legal system, every transgression has an applicable statute of limitations. The statute requires that a claim be filed within a prescribed period after the wrongful act was committed. The purpose is clear: To help ensure that claimants respond promptly in redressing wrongs, when evidence and witnesses' memories are fresh and available. There are certain instances where there is no statute of limitations, such as murder and other major crimes. But in all other instances timely notice is required; otherwise, the aggrieved party would be barred from making such claims.

Even a yacht race has a statute of limitations, albeit a very short one. If an infraction is committed on the racecourse, the yacht making a claim must hoist a protest flag in its starboard rigging and give notice to the race committee upon crossing the finish line of its intention to seek redress. No protest is permitted to be filed after the race is over.

Even though all the boats competing that week were prejudiced by this mistake, not one of the scores of sailors filed a protest after the race results. But how could we have detected the error? The IOR time allowance tables used for the races had never been posted by the Trysail Club. As a result, it was impossible for any of us to know that a mistake had been made by the race committee, so, of course, no protest was filed after the race. The posted results for every boat were wrong, but what could we do now?

At the time, I was commodore of MORC. I proposed a resolution to the board of governors barring the Block Island race results and declaring a "no race" due to the improper use of the time allowance tables. The resolution was passed unanimously, and the record books were corrected. But sadly, the *Sting Act II* could not be recorded as the winner, because we didn't officially win.

I knew that a strong legal case still could have been made to require the Trysail Club to change the race results, despite the statute of limitations. In the law there is a provision that permits the tolling of a statute of limitations when the damage is unknown and discovered only at a later date. When an error is actually *discovered*, a protest could be filed. In this case, a lawsuit would have been brought to force a recalculation of the race results, after the error was detected months later. As an aggrieved racing sailor—and as a lawyer—I had a decision to make. I understood that lawyers are often treated differently from other professionals because of their ready access to the legal system—sometimes to their benefit, sometimes not.

In my early thirties, for example, I developed a complicated tax plan for one of my clients who had undertaken a new project. The plan would greatly benefit him, if he was willing to create a company and carry out the project as a business. He liked the plan and was willing to go forward, but only if I would become president and manage the operation. Since he permitted me to maintain a small private law practice, I agreed. He also purchased a $10 million life insurance policy on me with him as the beneficiary in the event of my death.

Of course, I needed an extensive medical examination for him to obtain the policy. During the exam, a hilar shadow was detected in a lung's root area. After several months of testing, the doctor pronounced that he was "morally certain" that I was healthy. "Morally certain?" I wasn't interested in moral certainty; I wanted a medical opinion. When I pressed him, he said he knew I was a lawyer, and because of that, his language was intentionally guarded.

In other instances, I found that the appearance of a lawyer sometimes could prevent differences from arising, and even after they arose, a lawyer's presence could have a quieting effect. Such was the case with Ted Turner in 1970 when he was mounting his defense of the America's Cup, which he won for the United States as skipper of the yacht *Courageous*. During the elimination races his mast was damaged, and since Ted still had to complete the preliminary races, he asked the New York Yacht Club to use its influence in securing a backup mast from the other contestants.

There was little affection, however, between the established members of the genteel private club and the brash media entrepreneur, Turner. The club refused to exert its authority over the matter, putting Turner in a disastrous position, since he would be unable to get a new mast in time to compete in the next trial. So Ted pressed his position. He asked his navigator, Bill Jorch (a client of mine), for the name of a good lawyer. Bill gave him my name and that of my partner, Jerry Sullivan, who was known as the prosecutor in the Ronald DeFeo murder case that later became the basis for the *Amityville Horror* movie. Jerry and I immediately sought to file a civil action in federal court to compel the use of the mast held in reserve. When word circulated that Turner was preparing for litigation, lo and behold, the matter was amicably resolved, shortly after we arrived in Newport for the preliminary races.

In this case, the mere presence of a lawyer from New York, with the accompanying bad publicity, forced a solution. But the case of the *Sting Act II* was different. In the spirit of Corinthian yacht racing (and since we were an all-amateur boat and crew) we had only bragging rights to lose. The decision was easy to make: Let's not embarrass the race committee or make a mess of our sport with lawsuits. During my career spanning sixty years, I had a similar resolve: never to be a plaintiff on my own behalf. Either I settled the case or I walked away from my rights.

In the end, we didn't win the Block Island regatta, but we didn't lose, either. And now we were off to the international Midget Ocean Racing Club championship regatta with renewed confidence. The international regatta was uneventful, compared with Block Island Race Week. We attempted no death-defying navigational tactics on the racecourse. We sailed fast and won the international trophy.

Later that fall, we looked back on a campaign of great success – and a good deal of drama, which made it easy to remember, even after forty-plus years. We flew the Northport Yacht Club burgee all the way, and it was indeed a success for the club. With a crew of sailors from both the eastern and the western shore of Northport harbor, it was also a success for our home port: a memorable triumph for this team of great sailors, including Bill Jorch, Ron Lange, Paul Cavanagh, Ian McKecknie, Glenn Maaser and Manny Michaels, as well as Don Condit, the head sailing instructor at Northport Yacht Club, who was involved in the early days of the *Sting Act II*'s construction.

Oh, yes, there was another lasting outcome of the Block Island regatta. Because of the *Sting Act II*'s unique design, we were able to win the around-the-island race by skimming over the reef on the northern ledge of the island on the inland side of buoy 1Bl and cutting a significant distance off the racecourse, as described earlier. In future years, racing boats would have to stay seaward of the buoy 1B1. There would be no more reef skimming.

The following summer brought more adventures and the end of my racing career. I navigated the MORC international championship to a first-place finish and then sailed in the Chesapeake Fall Series to victory with Bill Jorch on Ted Turner's boat. MORC elected me to its Yacht Racing Hall of Fame. And finally, I took a deep breath and returned from the adrenaline of sailboat racing to the relative calm of practicing law.

9

Freeman McNeil

*An All-Pro New York Jet who stared down the
National Football League and changed free agency
forever*

"Are you Tony Curto the lawyer, or are you the person
Tony Curto?"

That was the paradoxical question Freeman McNeil
asked me in the summer of 1992. It was just after Freeman,
a star running back with the New York Jets, had spent hours
being grilled on the witness stand during a landmark lawsuit
challenging the fairness of the National Football League's
free agency policy. I was co-counsel in this case, representing
Freeman and seven other players, but I was also being called,
personally, to testify as an expert witness.

I was next up on the witness stand. While lawyers have
little difficulty submitting their clients to courtroom inter-
rogations, it's a different story when lawyers themselves
must testify. They get a chance to experience first-hand the

butterflies all witnesses feel. Freeman, sensing my tension, presented his guiding question: Would I be testifying as a lawyer, or as a person who happened to be a lawyer? I would have to choose.

The lawsuit had begun several years earlier, when I received a call at home one Saturday morning from Jim Quinn, a senior member of the premier New York law firm Weil, Gotshal & Manges, and head of the firm's litigation department. One of the most accomplished trial, arbitration and mediation lawyers in the country, Jim was preparing to file a lawsuit, along with the general counsel for the NFL Players Association, Dick Berthelsen. The suit alleged that the NFL's free agency system substantially harmed free competition for players' services, thus violating federal antitrust laws.

Jim and Dick were looking for a superstar to include among the handful of players specifically named in the lawsuit, someone who had been recently affected by the NFL's policy on free agency: Freeman McNeil. They saw Freeman—who was already my client—as the ideal plaintiff to bring suit against the NFL. And yes, they appreciated the historic symbolism in Freeman's name. As Jim recalled years later, Freeman told Dick: "I just want to leave something to the game I got so much out of. If it is a matter of standing up for something that I believe in, then that is what it takes."

In that brief telephone call, the die was cast. We agreed that Freeman's name would be listed first on the complaint so the case would be Freeman McNeil v. National Football League. Jim would be the suit's lead attorney and I would act as co-counsel, also giving expert testimony on the negotiating rights of players under the NFL's restrictive collective bargaining agreement.

The case of McNeil v. National Football League was originally filed in the United States District Court in New

Jersey but ended up being transferred to Minnesota. As it turned out, the Minnesota federal court had a relatively short calendar compared to those of other states, enabling us to get to trial quicker; it could have taken two or three times longer in a more congested court. The jury was made up of eight women—no men.

At 5 feet, 11 inches, 216 pounds, Freeman McNeil was a beautiful man, with milk-chocolate-brown skin as smooth as marble. He was picked by the Jets in the first round of the 1981 draft. Over twelve seasons, No. 24 was elected to the Pro Bowl and All-Pro teams three times. In 1982 he was the rushing leader in the NFL and became a member of the Jets' "Two-Headed Monster" backfield along with Johnny Hector, the other of the league's elite tandem. When Freeman retired, he was the leading rusher in Jets history, having amassed 8,074 yards from the line of scrimmage.

Having played hockey, lacrosse and football during my school days, I was no stranger to contact sports. But when watching players during NFL games, standing on the sidelines, I was simply stunned. It was frightening to be so close to the explosive collisions between these superb athletes— massive bodies, between 220 and 400 pounds, crashing into one another at great speed. The crowned football fields were designed to shed water, but they also resulted in players running downhill to the sidelines. I was absolutely intimidated. I felt fragile—in mortal danger!

But when the physical violence on the field was finished, Freemen was *the* ideal player in the eyes of the fans, always making time to sign autographs and engage in conversations with the media, his teammates and anybody else interested in football. He never revealed an inflated ego—and that would have been easy for someone accustomed to performing in front of seventy-thousand rabid fans.

Freeman carried himself with consummate grace and dignity. He was a friend of singer/songwriter Harry Chapin and his wife, Sandy, who were also my clients and close friends. The couple would often invite him to their house in Huntington when they were having fundraisers for local arts organizations. These were usually daytime affairs with lots of children. The children would all congregate around Freeman, sitting on the floor. Toward evening, he moved into Harry's study with kids in tow, closed the door and dimmed the lights. Then he would tell ghost stories. I watched the kids clutch one another in fright as the tales unfolded. How odd it was to see one of football's biggest stars, known for excelling at a violent sport, spinning spooky tales to little children in such a loving way. At the end of his storytelling, Freeman would hug them all, and they would always remember how No. 24 became their friend.

Freeman's seventh season, in 1987, was a very productive year, and the Jets signaled that they wanted to renew his contract. The president of the team, Steve Gutman, was in charge of player contracts—and he was also one of the toughest negotiators in the league. Steve had not only all of Freeman's performance statistics at his disposal but also a database of information with the comparative performances of all running backs in the league and their compensation.

I knew Steve would ask me what Freeman wanted for a five-year contract renewal. I believed it was best to keep negotiations simple: Make a monetary demand based solely Freeman's stats, which were certainly impressive. After discussing the matter with Freeman, he suggested five million dollars (the equivalent of a twenty-five-million-dollar demand today). When I asked Freeman why that figure came to mind, he said, "Because I have my heart set on it." I loved that response. So when Steve asked me how I came to that number, I simply repeated to him what Freeman said to me: "He has his heart set on it."

Steve countered with a story that occurred the prior season, when Freeman had blocked a linebacker—a highly touted rookie—and as result of the impact, the rookie blew out his knee. Watching the player writhing in pain, Freeman knew that he might have ended the kid's bright future. He was so affected that he took himself out of the game. Steve thought this was a breach of Freeman's responsibility to the team and pronounced that he would take this incident into consideration when responding to Freeman's salary demand.

I saw Freeman's action as just the opposite. His decision to take himself out of the game was in no way a breach of responsibility; it was a recognition of how issues like this *transcended* the game. And that's what I told Steve Gutman: Freeman's act was a credit not only to himself but also to his team, and to the National Football League. I pointed out that the Nuremberg trials did not accept *performance of duty* as an acceptable excuse when humanitarian issues were at stake. Freeman's decision to take a moment to collect himself was a statement that honored the higher instincts that we, as human beings, possess.

Freeman got his five million.

Despite the physical fury required to succeed in the NFL, I never saw Freeman angry. I did see him get upset—for example, the time he was on the witness stand being cross-examined by Frank Rothman, the powerhouse counsel for the NFL. In his typical style, Frank pressed Freeman with question after question, hammering his claim that the league's free agency policy was unfair to him and other players. The cross-examination lasted over two hours, in a case that would be filled with memorable drama. Rothman pointed out that Freeman had acknowledged that he was happy with his contract with the Jets, so there was really no reason for him to be in this courtroom, was there? But then, as Jim Quinn recalled in his book, *Don't Be Afraid to Win*, Rothman stepped over the line, accusing Freeman of being greedy.

"Well, Mr. Rothman," Freeman responded. "Let me put it like this: If you think giving a person money will make up for restricting that person—do you think that is fair, sir? I don't. I am asking for the right to make a choice." There was not much left for Frank to say. A few minutes later, he returned to his seat.

After Freeman testified, the judge called a brief recess. When we returned to the courtroom, I had some time to prepare for my upcoming testimony, knowing that judges almost never returned exactly on schedule. I was sitting directly behind Frank Rothman, and I believe he sensed my presence. He looked over his shoulder and then turned around in his swivel chair and stared directly at me. It reminded me of the stare-down before a heavyweight prize fight. I narrowed my eyes and returned the stare. Neither of us blinked for several minutes. Then someone approached Rothman with a question, and he turned his eyes away. The contest ended, I think, in a draw. Just then, the judge entered the courtroom and I was called to testify.

With Freeman's paradoxical question in mind, I took the stand. I was testifying not in my capacity as a lawyer, but as Tony Curto, the lawyer who was a widely recognized expert on the rights of contracted individuals with special talents who provided "unique services." Over the years, I had nego-tiated contracts for many high-profile clients with such tal-ents. Thus, I was qualified to render expert testimony about the fairness (or lack thereof) of the NFL's Plan B Free Agency policy, and its impact on the players.

Essentially, Plan B was a small version of free agency that the NFL granted after the player strike in 1987. The players had gone on strike because they were unhappy with their union's collective bargaining agreement with the league, which forced teams to compensate a team when that team lost a free agent. Under Plan B, teams were allowed to hold the rights to thirty-seven of their own players. If those players wanted to sign with another team, their current team would have the first crack at signing them, or the new club would be forced to compensate the old team. Anyone else could be an unencumbered free agent. It was a great plan, unless you happened to be one of those thirty-seven players on a team—like Freeman.

As I walked to the witness chair, I could feel Rothman's eyes on me, a new round of staring. I waited until I was sworn in, and then I fixed my eyes on Frank. Initially, he asked about my credentials, delving into various contracts I had negotiated for people with "special talent." He was an experienced litigator, and as he proceeded, I could feel him establishing a rhythm and pace to his questions. I was on the stand about an hour when his intensity and pace changed. We were approaching the noon lunch break. His voice grew louder; his pace quickened.

"Mr. Curto, did you have any problem requesting the Jets pay Mr. McNeil five million? Did anybody stop you? Isn't that a fair process? Isn't a negotiation a two-way street? Isn't it? Come on, Mr. Curto, isn't it a two-way street?"

I paused. Then: "Yes, Mr. Rothman, it *is* a two-way street. With four lanes in one direction and one in the other."

Tony the person showed up. As Jim Quinn put it in his book, "Another shut-down answer. Rothman had no further questions for Curto either." Witness dismissed.

The all-women jury, when questioned, acknowledged that they were not sports fans. This elicited a number of caustic comments, one by Pat Bowlen, the owner of the Denver Broncos, who said he did not want the future of the

NFL in the hands of "housewives." (Not surprisingly, this provoked a backlash from women's organizations around the country.) During thirty-six days of testimony, none of the owners had spoken up. It was a glaring omission that Jim Quinn pointed out in his closing argument: "Not one of them would make the walk up to the witness stand."

During the trial I spent many hours with counsel for the players, as well as their union representatives. I developed a friendship with Gene Upshaw, the executive director of the National Football League Players Association. As the jury was deliberating, we would pass the time playing cards. We had money, but no chips, so we used matches. When word came that the jury had reached a verdict, Upshaw grabbed the pot and the matches and flew out the door. Who is going to argue with a huge ex-football player? But he still took a lot of good-natured ribbing from the legal team in the days that followed—think Gene got more than he bargained for!

After three days of deliberation, the jury came back on September 10, 1992, with a unanimous verdict in favor of the players. Although the litigation was long and difficult, the results were clear: The landscape of the NFL had forever changed. The court had ruled that competition was the best and fairest way to determine salaries. It was clearly the wave of the future.

The success of the case was immediately evident. Even before the ink was dry on the decision, the contracts of several players were negotiated more favorably than they would have been under the previous system. Competition for players' services obviously increased their compensation, but when Freeman was interviewed by *The New York Times* he repeated what he said on the witness stand: It was all about freedom, not money. No amount of earnings—whether for him or for any other NFL player—equaled the freedom to pursue their careers in a free market.

Jim Quinn—the singular energy that brought the McNeil case to a successful conclusion—would continue to build his considerable reputation in the world of sports. He battled with owners in all four major sports leagues—the National Football League, the National Basketball Association, Major League Baseball and the National Hockey League—to make sure the players got their fair share.

Nevertheless, over the years, there have been dozens of sad stories about the loss of wealth, health and friendships among pro athletes. From a young age, many outstanding athletes from low socioeconomic backgrounds are identified as gifted. As they are catapulted into professional sports, they are pampered in many ways, but little is done to help them develop life skills outside sports. As a result, they become easy prey to all sorts of bad influences. I was not going to let this happen to Freeman McNeil. I surrounded him with an accountant, an investment advisor, lawyers, an insurance agent and a Roman Catholic priest. They would become Freeman's personal team, devoted to his well-being and success. At the end of his last contract Freeman was offered an extension, but after much discussion, he decided to end his career, with the full approval of his team. Having participated in contact sports myself, I was well aware of the physical consequences of playing football. Pro athletes are in agreement that after every weekend they feel as if they've come out of a car crash.

Today, some two thousand players are experiencing this kind of physical beating in the pros every year, and another ten thousand athletes play on college and high school teams. Watching Freeman McNeil in his playing days, I knew then that the human body could never withstand this kind of continuous punishment. I could easily envision the broken bodies, the suffering from injuries to the neck, spinal column, hips and knees.

What I did not envision (and neither did many experts) was the lasting effect that concussions would have on these players. There is now well-established science showing that playing football can lead to lasting brain damage, although the implications are still barely understood, given the short period of study. To be certain, the problem is increasing, because of the athleticism of football players and the level of coaching and conditioning, which have improved beyond anything ever anticipated. It has become, in and of itself, a medical plague.

Like many other retired pro football players, Freeman McNeil is suffering from CTE, or chronic traumatic encephalopathy. On several occasions he has been involuntarily committed to hospital psychiatric wards. He has joined a class action lawsuit of football players making claims against the NFL for these life-changing injuries. With medication, he can live a normal life—provided his condition does not get worse. Current evidence suggests that it will.

Freeman will always be recognized as one of the best running backs in NFL history, but his greater legacy is what he accomplished off the field. As Boomer Esiason, the former New York Jets quarterback and sports commentator, once noted, Freeman "paved the way for a lot of players. He put his reputation, his name and his face on the line."

Because of the relationship I established with sports leaders, I was in a good position over the course of my career to build a significant practice representing professional athletes, especially football players. But I decided to represent only one athlete.

I'm thankful it was Freeman McNeil.

10

Kevin O'Neill

*The ex-Wall Streeter who came to a small town to
revive a theater and transformed a community along
the way*

From his early years as a kid selling lemonade on a street
corner in Brooklyn, Kevin O'Neill had the heart of an
entrepreneur.

As a teenager, Kevin worked alongside his mother and
father in their liquor store, where he acquired a respect for
customers and learned what was required to keep them coming back. During his college years at Fordham, he became
director of the student deli and doubled its sales.

After graduation, Kevin was offered a position at Salomon Brothers, one of the premier investment houses on Wall
Street—but getting the offer wasn't so easy. Fordham was a
fine university, but the networking opportunities that provide entrée to an elite Wall Street firm weren't readily available. Each year, 10,000 college graduates apply to Salomon

Brothers for a job and only one percent of those applicants survive the gauntlet of four rounds of interviews. Initially, Kevin was turned down, but with his characteristic refusal to give up, he appealed his case and finally pried the door open. Once on the job, he distinguished himself, and by the early 2000s Kevin had climbed up through the fiercely competitive ranks to become a senior bond trader. On any given day he would pick up the phone dozens of times and execute hundreds of transactions, buying and selling billions of dollars' worth of U.S. Treasury bonds.

Kevin was athletic and good looking, with a fair complexion and fading adult freckles that revealed his Irish ancestry. He was well suited for this high-pressure Wall Street environment where young, smart, energetic people had to make quick decisions, often based on instinct. But after several years, it became clear that he was putting his health at risk. With his family—life, Patti, and four children—living in Huntington, Long Island, he knew it was time to find a new line of work that was less stressful and closer to home. It didn't matter if he knew anything about the business; he had absolute confidence that in a relatively short time he would figure out all its needs.

He decided to invest in an online theater marketing company, and he learned of a troubled old movie house that was up for sale. Located in the historic waterfront village of Northport, on Long Island's North Shore, the theater was the kind of place that had a balcony where local teenagers fell in love—or thought they had.

I knew Northport well. The first time I sailed into Northport Harbor. more than fifty years ago, I decided that this would be the place I would settle down in and raise my family. Northport was a lovely harborside village, with good schools, quaint shops and storefronts, numerous Victorian houses and old trolley tracks still in place—the quintessential suburban community, with real ties to the past—very different from many towns that had sprung up on Long Island after World War II.

The first Europeans came to this area in 1650, and it soon became a busy whaling center, launching ships that would travel the globe seeking whale blubber, which took them away for years on end. Like that of most small Long Island towns in the 1800s, Northport's economy relied on waterfront-related businesses like shipbuilding, oyster farming and sand mining. But at the end of the century, the village also became a major hub for legal publishing with the founding of the Edward Thompson Company. The company became widely known for publishing *The American and English Encyclopedia of Law*, the country's first legal encyclopedia, as well as many other volumes, including *McKinney's Consolidated Laws of New York*.

In 1935, when his publishing business was sold to West Publishing, Edward Thompson moved to Brooklyn. Thompson's building in downtown Northport was eventually bought by Davis Aircraft Products Co., founded by the prolific Long Island inventor Frank L. Davis. Perhaps best known as the developer of the first seatbelts used in cars and airplanes, David Aircraft became a major manufacturer of seatbelts for commercial and military airplanes, eventually moving its operations to Bohemia, Long Island.

Of course, Northport also garnered some short-lived notoriety during the late 1950s and early 1960s, when the famous beat-generation novelist and poet Jack Kerouac lived there with his mother. Kerouac had moved to Northport in an attempt to escape the fan frenzy created by his best-selling novel, *On the Road*. He was known frequently to hold court well into the morning at Gunther's Tap Room on Main Street, until he moved to Florida in 1964. During the post-Kerouac era, Northport remained a lovely but stagnant twentieth century village; it needed to find a twenty-first-century identity.

Then along came Kevin O'Neill.

Before Kevin decided to buy the Northport Theater in 2006, it was not much to look at, known mostly for showing second-run movies at cut-rate prices. The building that housed the original movie theater was constructed in 1912 and used to show silent films, in addition to hosting high school graduation ceremonies, political rallies, music recitals and even basketball games. When the building was destroyed by fire, it was rebuilt on the adjoining lot in 1932. In subsequent decades, the fireproof building underwent multiple alterations and ownerships.

Once he bought the building, Kevin knew he would have to invest several million dollars more to renovate the theater. But Kevin was not interested simply in renovation; he was interested in *transformation*.

Kevin wanted to reinvent the old movie house as a venue that could produce live, professional theater performances for sophisticated suburban audiences that did not want to trek into New York City to enjoy Broadway-caliber shows. It was not to be a dalliance into nonprofit amateur theater by a successful ex-Wall Streeter looking for a hobby. Kevin wanted to create a successful marriage of money and the arts—and to improve the community in the process. Years later, he would describe his theater in simple terms: "We're a for-profit. We do well or we close."

Kevin wasn't a regular theatergoer when he entered the business, so he needed to figure out what was involved in putting on a show. While most movie theaters did not have a stage suitable for presentation of live shows, this old place had a presidium stage, with enough depth and width in its wings to support the physical requirements to put on a show. That was a good start. But what would it take for this broken-down movie theater to be resurrected into a quality, performing arts community theater?

That's when Kevin's entrepreneurial instincts kicked in. He started to ask a lot of questions that needed answers, and he needed to find the right people to answer them before he could go forward. The central questions:

- How much of the building had to be destroyed and how much could be saved?
- How much money would it take carry out the restoration?
- Do I need any local government approvals or permits?
- What are the union costs?
- What about seating, acoustics, lighting? How much would all that cost?
- Most important, how does one bring a Broadway revival to this Northport theater?
- What kind of shows could be produced, and assuming their success, would they result in *financial success?*

Like other entrepreneurs, Kevin knew that he could not accomplish great things alone; he would need to assemble a group of talented people around him. Besides new restaurants, no new enterprise fails more often than newly formed theater groups. These startups are usually driven by people in love with the arts, but their love for the theater is not enough to make these ventures successful financially. It takes adequate capital, administrative experience and management capable of working with lawyers, accountants, architects, construction people, audio and sound engineers and, of course, actors and musicians. It also takes a first-class product that will excite local theatergoers.

Patti, his wife, was committed to the project, but he needed a theatrical person who had the expertise to select and manage shows that would appeal to the largest audiences possible.

Enter Richard Dolce, stage right.

Richard Dolce had a Lincolnesque, calming presence; he had earned degrees in both accounting and law. On top of that, he had lifelong love of the theater, having helped run his family's nonprofit Broadhollow Theatre Company, which today has performance spaces in East Islip, Lindenhurst and Elmont, Long Island. When they met, Kevin and Richard immediately liked each other. They had mutual respect, and a bond of trust quickly evolved as they discussed the project and problems they could face over lunches at the local diner. Six months after their first meeting, Kevin decided to buy the theater, having come to believe that Dolce was the missing piece, the partner he needed for his enterprise to succeed.

As managing director, Kevin would give Richard a quality showcase where he could demonstrate his artistic skills with outstanding theater decor, blending many of the old movie house's qualities with state-of-the-art audio and lighting appointments that made the theater a gem. Kevin's job would be to find ways to fill the theater; Richard's job would be to entertain its patrons so they would come back, again and again. As Kevin would say, "What good is an empty theater?"

Richard was a first-rate artistic director. He had a gift for knowing what Long Islanders wanted, and he gave it to them: impeccably directed shows that were suited to the theater as well as Long Island audiences. Show selection, talent, costuming and set construction were among the challenges that Richard handled, all to good and often great reviews from critics.

Rebranding the old Northport movie house required coming up with a new name. While Kevin was considering the purchase of the theater, his brother-in-law, John Engeman, a soldier in Iraq, was killed by a bomb that exploded near his Humvee. John had served in the Army for over twenty-eight years in multiple deployments, and at the time of his death—on Mother's Day, 2006—he was assisting the Iraqi people in establishing their own security forces. The Iraqis honored John by placing his biography and picture in the Iraqi Hall of Martyrs.

Closer to home, Kevin and Patti were looking for a memorial to honor John's life, but also to serve as a reminder to the community of the ultimate sacrifice that local men and women were making in answering their country's call. John himself had enjoyed the theater and had been involved in high school while growing up in East Northport and later in the Army while stationed in Germany. And so, the John W. Engeman Theater at Northport would become the perfect tribute to a lost soldier.

Kevin worked day and night, putting all the pieces together to turn his kernel of an idea into reality. The result was a first-rate playhouse, which opened in 2007, offering theatrical experiences usually available only in larger cities. Kevin built a piano lounge and wood-paneled bar in the lobby of the theater, dubbed the Green Room. The stadium-style seating provided 402 seats, all with cupholders for drinks, and seat-side beverage service as well. Kevin arranged for valet parking, a major convenience for suburban theater-goers, who could now have a great experience from curbside to curtain.

Today, Engeman Theater performers are all Broadway tested and union blessed. Actors often stay after the show and take advantage of the piano in the lobby to keep the night's entertainment going. Kevin bought a van to provide transportation for actors going to and from the city, and when it's not in use he lends out the van to worthy community causes. In between shows, as the theater is gearing up for its next production, major performers from New York are invited to perform songs they sang on Broadway in an "unplugged" fashion.

Kevin's mind has never been in idle. Step by step, he has demonstrated the benefit to the community of having a theater as one of its main attractions. Kevin set off selling sponsorships to banks, hospitals and law firms, and attracted local patrons of the arts who would be loyal to his new endeavor. He started workshops and children's theater productions to round out the theatrical experience. He made the theater available to local fund-raising groups, with the theater itself doing its share to help raise money. Through his strategic marriage of business, the arts and the community, Kevin created a transformative venue that now brings in over a hundred thousand visitors every year to this village of just seven-thousand-plus residents.

I had met Kevin one day at a local small business expo, where I complimented him on the work he had been doing in Northport. Over the years I had assumed various leadership roles in the community, because I loved what it meant to the families who lived there and in neighboring towns. Kevin and I enjoyed each other's company, and he asked whether he could use me as a resource. "By all means," I said. I also bought season tickets.

Over the next several years I worked regularly with Kevin, *pro bono*, on matters involving unions, zoning, financial structure, a range of activities and problems associated with the village and finally, the structuring of investor participation for an ambitious new venture being undertaken by Kevin and Richard—hotel and restaurant, located on Main Street across from the theater.

At this writing, the partners are building the North-port Hotel, an upscale, twenty-four-room inn inspired by the likes of inns in the seaside towns of Maine and the American Hotel in Sag Harbor on Long Island's East End. The first floor of the hotel, which is replacing an old three-story office building, features a white-tablecloth, 125-seat restaurant with a 50-seat bar. In addition, Kevin is working with government officials to fund a massive sewer system to alleviate flooding that regularly plagues downtown streets during heavy rains.

Along with the theater, this venue will complete a cultural package that will make the village a weekend destination spot, whether by boat or by car. The overall improvements will lift real estate and businesses values; provide accommodations in an area vastly underserved in lodging; and elevate this seaside community to a model for many other towns to follow.

Kevin has become a builder who knows how to make money while creating a new vision for his village. But he has never been a detached thinker who develops a master plan and then hands it off to local politicians or other business interests. He creates his vision in pieces, crystalizing his plan as he shares ideas with the people around him. He's a hands-on entrepreneur—a builder-owner-operator, not a "builder-leaver." When the old office building was being taken down to make room for his hotel, for example, Kevin was not watching the demolition from his office. He was working in the street, in hardhat and work clothes, helping the construction crew drill steel girders into the ground to support the new structure.

Given all the challenges Kevin has faced, his success as a civic-minded entrepreneur is an extraordinary achievement. But what has made his story even more remarkable is the physical obstacles he has had overcome to make this project a success.

During the ten-plus years he's been working on this enterprise, there has never been a day where Kevin was able to work without pain. As a teenager, he was thrown through the windshield of his friend's car, in which he was a passenger. After the accident, he went through nine major spinal operations. Many times, doctors refused to do such operations because they believed they were too dangerous and could leave him paralyzed for life.

Kevin traveled to hospitals all over the country in search of a surgical treatment that could eliminate the constant pain. Today he relies on painkillers and an electronic nerve suppressor that was surgically embedded in his spine. As the pain increases, he increases the supply of electronic suppressing stimuli to help him make it through the day.

So as Kevin O'Neill tackles problem after problem, his focus is always compromised by pain, which he handles by realizing his vision to create a successful business entity devoted to the performing arts while enhancing the community. To accomplish what he does under such circumstances is indeed an epic entrepreneurial triumph.

11

Charlie Ferro

*The soda guy who propelled C&C Cola and Yoo-hoo
to national brands and, oh, yeah, inherited Yogi, too*

On a Sunday morning in the fall of 1963, on my way to a New York Giants game with a client, we stopped at a beer and soda distributorship on Jericho Turnpike on Long Island. It was there that I met Gaspare Ferro—Charlie, to everyone who knew him. This was the beginning of more than half a century working with this extraordinary "serial entrepreneur."

Charlie started out as the owner of a single beer and soda distributorship and then propelled beverages like C&C Cola and Yoo-hoo into wildly popular brands known across America. Charlie and his partner, Al Di Pasqua, would become legends in the soft drink business, and my relationship with Charlie, both professionally and personally, was one of the most rewarding of my life.

On that football Sunday, my client, Russell Merket, who had purchased a beer and soda distributorship in nearby Valley Stream, was thinking about joining a venture called Thrifty Beverage Centers of Long Island. Russ invited me to hear the organization's business proposition. The storefront was closed, but inside was a group of maybe two dozen independent beer and soda distributors from different parts of the Island, sitting around on beer cases. I took a seat in the back of the room.

It wasn't long before a diminutive, well-groomed man with sharp and distinctive features stood up in front of the group and started to outline his plan for buying and selling beverages on Long Island. After a few minutes, his eyes caught mine and he abruptly stopped. "Who are you?" he demanded. I said my friend Russ had invited me to come to the meeting before we headed out to the Giants game. With an air of self-assuredness that I soon discovered to be his trademark, Charlie Ferro threw me out of the meeting. He sent me packing to the warehouse, some distance away.

About half an hour later, however, Russ summoned me back in. A legal question had come up. and Russ had told the group that since I was a lawyer, perhaps I could help. A few minutes later, I was representing these two dozen distributors, who had joined together to form Thrifty Beverage Centers of Long Island.

Charlie was what I call a pure entrepreneur. He did not fit into any box. He was a free thinker, and he was never going to work for anyone else. He didn't think much of the stock market, where an eight percent return couldn't compare with the money he could make by creating or acquiring companies, building them into highly successful enterprises and then selling them.

Charlie's family members were always employed in their own businesses, so it was natural for him to follow in their footsteps. Charlie first worked for his father's taxi business, but he soon decided to strike out on his own. His first venture was a small beverage distributorship in Garden City Park on Long Island. It was here that Charlie began to educate himself about consumers, learning how they thought, how they functioned, how savvy they were. His respect for them continued to grow over the years. He believed the customer was always the "smartest guy in the room. You can't fool 'em."

While Charlie gained a keen understanding of his customers, he soon realized he was facing a major challenge in the local market. His chief competition wasn't other beer and soda distributorships; it was the big supermarkets. Charlie couldn't compete on price with those stores because he didn't have their buying power, sales volume or advertising budget. But Charlie believed that if he could bring together the small, independent distributors as a cooperative enterprise, they could effectively compete with the supermarkets. By pooling their funds, they could purchase greater volumes of products at lower prices and promote them through a joint advertising campaign, each store paying its fair share. These small stores were located in different areas, so they wouldn't compete with each other.

This was the plan Charlie presented to the group of distributors who met with him in the fall of 1963. It was not a unique business model, but it was unique to the beverage industry, especially to independent distributors. It was a simple concept, yet it would substantially increase their profits and sales volume, taking away the formidable competitive advantage of the supermarkets.

Thrifty Beverage Centers of Long Island soon became a huge success. But that was just the first mountain Charlie had to climb. While he held his ground against the supermarkets, he realized he still could not compete on price with big national brands like Coke and Pepsi. These two companies had been slugging it out for more than half a century, manufacturing and selling their own products. Charlie was buying products from them, so clearly, he could not undersell them. He believed that his group would do better with a "vertical dollar," manufacturing its own label. It was time for the Thrifty Beverage group to produce a cola of its own.

After some research, Charlie and his partner, Al Di Pasqua, discovered an obscure brand called Cantrell & Cochrane, which dated back to a company founded in Belfast, Ireland, in 1865. After moving to a manufacturing plant in America in 1955, the company became known for its cone-top cans, which were lighter and more economical than glass bottles; they were eventually upgraded to flat-top cans.

Charlie and Al decided to buy the Cantrell & Cochrane brand and a bottling factory in New Jersey. Instead of raising capital for the purchase through the usual route, a public stock offering, they decided to pitch the beer and soda guys who had joined Thrifty Beverage, asking them to become investors in return for equity participation in the company. Most of them signed on.

After buying Cantrell & Cochrane, Charlie shortened the brand name to C&C Cola and hired a master flavor chemist, John Ritchie, the inventor of the Pepsi formula, to create a new flavor for their own cola. C&C blitzed the soft drink market with the catchy slogan "A cola as good as Coke and Pepsi. At about half the price." Ingenious. Charlie's group now owned the product they sold, and it sold quite well, becoming the third-largest-selling cola in the regional markets where it was distributed—mainly metro New York, California, Florida and Pennsylvania. Charlie came to be known in the industry as "C&C Charlie."

In 1976, Charlie and Al Di Pasqua decided it was time to cash in on their investment and sell C&C Cola. I handled the negotiations with the buyer, ITT Corp., resulting in the sale of the company for about $13 million—no small sum of money at that time, and the equivalent of almost $60 million today. Half of the proceeds went to Charlie and Al; the other half went to about twenty Thrifty Beverage distributors, who got $300,00, $400,00 or more, depending on how much they had invested.

Al, following the advice of Bernard Baruch, the renowned financier whom I had represented a few years earlier, never risked his own capital again. As Baruch noted, "Nobody ever lost money taking a profit," and Al modestly managed his money and counseled other manufacturers in the soft drink industry.

For a few years Charlie worked as president of ITT's soft drink division, but it was not a good fit. ITT was a huge conglomerate intent on aggregating companies; Charlie was always focused on learning about customers. He was never happy unless he was working on some venture, looking for another mountain to climb. As I said, he was a pure entrepreneur.

Charlie once had an opportunity to buy Poland Spring, but he passed. (Who could predict that a gallon of water would someday cost more than a gallon of gas?) A year or so later, Charlie called me and said he was considering buying an interest in a chocolate drink known as Yoo-hoo. I knew Yoo-hoo. *Everyone* knew Yoo-hoo, which was famously promoted by the beloved New York Yankees catcher, Yogi Berra, and his teammates ("It's Me-he for You-hoo!").

Charlie had met a promoter named Al Hoffman, who told him that the Yoo-hoo Chocolate Beverage Co., then owned by Iroquois Brands Ltd., was for sale. Like C&C Cola, Yoo-hoo had a long history. The chocolate drink was invented by the owner of a small grocery store in New Jersey, Natale Olivieri, who started bottling carbonated fruit drinks in the mid-1920s. When he tried to bottle a chocolaty version of his juices, however, he found that it soon spoiled. His wife was using a heat-processing technique to can fruits and vegetables, so he asked her to try the same technique with his chocolate drink. It worked, and in 1928 Olivieri began bottling a pasteurized chocolate drink he named Yoo-hoo, like his other fruit drinks. In the late 1950s, BBC Industries bought the rights to Yoo-hoo. BBC, which distributed Yoo-hoo in the Bronx (and owned the New York fast-food restaurant Nedick's), retained ownership of Yoo-hoo until 1976, when it sold the brand to Iroquois.

Hoffman said he wanted to put together a team of investors and was looking for a "soda guy" with a reputation and experience in the industry—Charlie. Hoffman offered Charlie a ten percent interest in Yoo-hoo for half a million dollars in cash. I asked Al and his lawyer for copies of the proposed documents, but he told me he couldn't give them to me since they were being held in escrow. Armed with a bank check, Charlie and I traveled to Stamford, Connecticut, together with his accountant and trusted adviser, Ed Salzano, to negotiate the purchase of Yoo-hoo. When we arrived at Iroquois's office, we were ushered into the conference room; all the documents had been executed and sealed in escrow, pending payment.

On the fly, Ed Salzano and I sat down and reviewed the paperwork. It didn't take long to determine that Charlie was getting a ten percent interest for his investment, as promised—but his money was the only cash in the deal. The balance of the five-million-dollar purchase price was to be covered by the company taking back a note for a 4.5-million-dollar loan. Charlie and I realized that Al Hoffman's partners were actually "finders, not buyers." They were promoters, and as such, we believed that they were the party entitled to a ten percent ownership stake, while Charlie should own ninety percent of the company. I emphatically pointed out to Hoffman and his partners that without Charlie's money and knowledge of the beverage industry, there was no deal. Several hours of intense discussions followed, but they finally got it. Charlie walked out of the meeting with a ninety percent ownership in Yoo-hoo and Hoffman got a ten percent finder's fee.

Along with Yoo-hoo, we got Yogi.

Yogi Berra had been associated with Yoo-hoo for decades; in many quarters the brand was inseparable from the baseball player. Yogi reportedly had met two of Olivieri's children on a New Jersey country club golf course in 1955 and they hit it off. Yogi liked the family—and he loved Yoo-hoo.

Yogi soon began appearing in print ads for the chocolate drink, and he was made an honorary vice president without portfolio at the company. Yogi had taken on side ventures before, including a successful bowling alley in North Jersey he ran with his best friend, Yankee shortstop Phil Rizzuto. But this was a big step up: With his unique image, sometimes appearing with teammates like Mickey Mantle, Yogi became the face of Yoo-hoo. "Yogi and Yoo-hoo just seemed to make sense," Yankees pitcher Jim Bouton once told *The New York Times*. "We used to keep it in a cooler in the clubhouse."

Yogi's name, of course, had its own amusing origin story. At sixteen, he was playing in an American Legion game when his teammate, Bobby Hoffman (later a major league infielder), noticed that when Berra sat waiting to bat, arms and legs crossed, he looked like an Indian yogi in a movie Hoffman had seen. The nickname stuck, but it did not stop the slew of other insulting names hurled at Yogi from opposing players in his rookie year—everything from derogatory epithets (the Ape) to a host of Italian ethnic slurs.

Yogi brushed them off. He earned a reputation as an outstanding catcher and a superb hitter who also had the ability to frustrate opposing pitchers by hitting balls well out of the strike zone. Over the course of his career, he was all an All-Star for fifteen seasons and won the American League Most Valuable Player award three times. He appeared in fourteen World Series, winning ten championships. In his post-playing career, he had several managerial stints, for the Yankees, the New York Mets and the Houston Astros. His number 8 was retired by the Yankees, and he was inducted into the Hall of Fame in 1972.

Of course, Yogi also achieved iconic status as a pop culture figure for his "Yogi-isms": seemingly accidental witticisms, sometimes humorous contradictions that actually served up a pithy message. His most quoted Yogi-ism, "It ain't over till it's over," turned out to be a prescient one. He delivered it during the 1973 season, when the Mets were in last place in their division with a month to go in the regular season. Surprising all the pundits, they improbably won twenty-four of their last thirty-three games, surging past five teams to win the National League East division title.

Along the way, I witnessed several of Berra's Yogi-isms, as well as a few inside baseball stories, some funny, others a bit edgy. In his 1989 autobiography, *It Ain't Over*, Yogi offered this Yoo-hoo-specific story: "One time I was in the office and the phone rang when no one else was around. I always answer a ringing phone, so I did. The woman who was calling asked if Yoo-hoo was hyphenated. I said, 'No ma'am, it's not even carbonated.'"

When Charlie bought Yoo-hoo, Yogi reportedly owned a piece of the company. His Yogi-isms may have made people laugh, but he was a shrewd man and a hard bargainer.

Throughout his major league baseball career, he would hold out for raises, making him one of the three highest paid players at the time.

After the Yoo-hoo deal closed, I contacted Yogi and had several lengthy conversations with him. I thought he would be represented by his lawyer, but no, he handled the negotiations himself. Yogi was Yogi: sometimes very direct, sometimes hard to figure out, but always on point. He felt his name was as important as Yoo-hoo itself, and he wanted a comparable payday. After one long discussion, I finally got him to acknowledge that he would be better off making a deal for less money than no deal at all. I suggested that he sleep on it, and we'd regroup the following day. Yogi did sleep on it. But he called me the next day with the same request—more money.

In the end, we could not find a middle ground. After we parted ways, I ran into Yogi several times at local golf outings, where he was always affable, willing to discuss the matter, if we ever changed our minds. But Charlie was also firm. He had no trouble leaving people behind when deals did not work out. He broke down problems as if they we just a bunch of dry twigs that simply needed to be raked into a pile. He showed no emotion. I never heard him raise his voice; his language and demeanor were sparing and direct, although from time to time I would glimpse a sense of humor that revealed his human side.

Charlie kept a careful watch over his products and any potential competitors that might threaten them. He scanned the landscape of the beverage business and concluded that Yoo-hoo was the only *milk-based* chocolate drink that was made hydrostatically. All his competitors were chocolate drinks that were water based. Producing the milky nature of Yoo-hoo required a specific kind of cooking tower that was manufactured abroad and took several years' lead time to order and install. Charlie kept close tabs on this manufacturer. He knew that if anyone was thinking about bottling a pasteurized milk beverage, they would have to purchase such equipment well in advance of production, so he would easily be able to anticipate his competitors' moves.

Meanwhile, Charlie instructed his son, Pat—now a senior executive at the company—and me to buy up other chocolate drink labels that were available for purchase. Charlie never had any intention of marketing these brands. His strategy was simply to block competitors from buying name brands of chocolate drinks.

On one memorable excursion, we went to Boston, expecting to spend a day and stay overnight in a hotel after concluding deals to buy Moxi and Chocolate Soldier, two well-known chocolate brands. Instead, Pat and I found ourselves in a kind of kabuki dance that lasted several days, going up and down the hotel elevator, walking into negotiations, then out again when we ran into an impasse. Sometimes we would be called back by the sellers; sometimes we had to surrender our positions in order to move the deal along. Finally, we succeeded and returned to the plant, excited to report our hard-fought results to Charlie. He was only mildly impressed. I came to understand that Charlie was driven by *ideas*. The important thing here was creating the strategic plan to buy up competitors' brands; the process of buying them—well, that was just nuts-and-bolts stuff.

By the mid-1980s, Charlie had paid off the $4.5 million debt that the company owed to the sellers when he bought Yoo-hoo. Charlie also had bought out the stock positions of Al Hoffman and his partners. Pat, who was now playing a more significant role in the operations of the company, believed that Yoo-hoo's profits had peaked, that the value of the company had been fully realized. Pat noted that competitors were closely watching Yoo-hoo's success and would shortly be closing the gap in market share. Heeding Pat's advice, Charlie decided it was time to sell.

We contacted investment bankers to orchestrate the sale, and after considerable discussion, identified a handful of suitable buyers. The leading candidate was Pernod Ricard, a French conglomerate with a soft drink unit that was selling Orangina worldwide. Following several weeks of negotiations, ending with a day-and-night session where the deal appeared in jeopardy, a bargain was finally struck. My law partner, Barbara Alisi, and I concluded the transaction for a purchase price of more than one hundred million dollars, including a great deal of protection against any offsets to the purchase price. Besides the initial purchase price of half a million in cash, Charlie probably had invested about ten million dollars in growing Yoo-hoo. It took five and a half years and a lot of hard work, but Charlie and Pat ultimately won the day.

Looking back at all the entrepreneurs I represented in more than six decades of practice, there was no one more skilled than Charlie Ferro. He was an amazing theoretician: He would look at present market conditions and the product he wished to advance and then methodically move his company into the market. He was not the kind of man who liked to roll up his sleeves, walk into the warehouse and organize cases of beer. He saw his primary value as being the creative force behind the execution of strategic plans, to which he could assign people to get the job done.

Charlie was driven by a burning entrepreneurial spirit throughout his life, compelled to confront every mountain faced, climb it and move on to the next one. He spent all his time working at his businesses. I never saw him unfocused. But this unwavering commitment left him little time for anything else, and he inevitably paid a heavy price in his family relationships, as so many entrepreneurs do.

In his later years, Charlie retired to Boca Raton, Florida, where he built a beautiful home. One day, while discussing Charlie's estate plan, I suggested an idea that would not only address his tax concerns but keep his family together in the coming years: the creation of a charitable foundation in his name. Charlie was enthusiastic about the idea. If he created a foundation, his children and grandchildren, and the generations that followed, would have an opportunity to meet regularly and maintain some familial relationships, while also contributing to the good of society. Thus, the foundation was launched, with Charlie's three children bringing their own perspectives to the task of passing out monies to worthwhile causes.

Charlie Ferro passed away in 2001. Over the next two decades, his children have continued to make decisions together, advancing their charitable goals through the legacy of their father.

12

Bala

A tech genius who revolutionized the financial services industry but discovered that even moral victories can end in legal defeat

Self-starters come from all nationalities, races, ethnic groups and genders.

The capacity to dream—and to turn that dream into reality—isn't a gift conferred upon any singular demographic. You can find these individuals anywhere. To be sure, there are certain qualities that separate them from the rest of us. One such person I got to know was a first-generation American entrepreneur extraordinaire named Balkrishna Shagrithaya—Bala, for short.

Bala was tall for an Asian Indian, and graceful in his movements. He became my client though a notorious court case in Texas, which exemplified one of the lessons of entrepreneurism that I witnessed again and again during my career: that a moral victory, no matter how emphatic, can still end in legal defeat.

Born in Bombay (now Mumbai), India, Bala was the oldest child of a father who worked for the railroad and a stay-at-home mother with five other children to raise. The family lived in a two-room apartment, and by any standard measurement would have been considered poor. Bala advanced through school by winning scholarships and graduating from the internationally acclaimed engineering college, the Indian Institute of Technology Bombay.

Bala's next chapter was one of multiple choices, struggles and obstacles. Should he stay with his family in India and build his career there, choosing from the job offers he had in hand? Or should he seek other opportunities? Ultimately, Bala realized that his dream was to come to the United States and be in an environment where he could fully display his talents, even if it meant facing the unknown. He eventually found his way to Oklahoma State University, where he received a master's degree in industrial engineering and operations research. Along the way, he took every computer course available.

In 1970, Bala landed a job in RCA's computer software division, working on operating systems. At the time, RCA was making the Spectra 70 series of computers, which were largely IBM compatible. He then moved to Electronic Data Systems (EDS), the Texas-based multinational information technology company founded by Ross Perot. It was there that Bala met Max Martin.

After working at EDS for several years, Bala left the company to work in the technology group of an accounting firm. In 1980, Max asked Bala to join him in a startup company focused on providing software to banks and other financial services firms, employing computer programs that targeted customer usage. Over a kitchen table, with a thousand dollars in startup capital, the two friends formed Argo Data Resource Corp. At that meeting, Max discussed the need for one partner to have more than fifty percent of the company, in order to avoid potential impasses that could affect the company's future. Max, having had years of business experience, was persuasive. Bala, meanwhile, had the skills to develop the core technology, but little experience managing a business. He trusted Max, so he agreed to let him have fifty-three percent of the company, while he retained ownership of forty-seven percent Both were directors and had an equal vote, but in addition, Max also would have the authority to appoint a third director. Of course, in the event of a disagreement between Bala and Max, this third director would act under Max's direction, thereby securing his absolute control of the company. Thus, the structure of Argo was set: Max would be the sole majority shareholder, Bali the sole minority shareholder.

The first successful sale of their newly created system was to Whitney National Bank. Argo presented all their ideas on paper, landing the sale without the benefit of producing a working model to demonstrate that it actually worked—something that would be virtually impossible to do today. It was an immediate success, recognized as a valuable addition to consumer banking. Once their product had been accepted by a reputable bank like Whitney, the opportunity to render more comprehensive IT services to this bank and other banks became much more viable.

Next up: Wachovia Bank. Wachovia chose Argo over IBM to build their system—an impressive triumph. Thereafter, their reputation would spread as a firm that could employ complex data organizational retrieval techniques on multiple platforms, performing routine functions accurately and quickly. Argo installed its system in sixteen of the top thirty banks in the country. Max Martin and Bala Shagrithaya had established themselves as visionary pioneers in integrating complex interdepartmental functions that supported the administration of customer services. Their systems, the guts of the company's enterprise, were all designed by Bala, who was recognized as Argo's brain trust.

Initially, the two men agreed to take no salary and issue no dividends to themselves as shareholders, investing their earnings in the company with the goal of growing the business. And grow they did! Through the business acumen of Max Martin and the technological savvy of Bala, Argo's value rose from $1,000 to well over $2.5 million in about twenty-five years, becoming one of the most successful tech companies servicing the financial industry. While the salaries of the founders gradually increased to $1 million apiece, Argo accumulated $152 million in after-tax capital. In fact, when the IRS audited Argo for the 2005 tax year, it imposed a penalty on the company for excessive retained earnings—penalty the company successfully protested.

During the early 2000s, however, the relationship between the two partners began to fray. Martin began pressing Bala to give up his responsibility for creating products and expand his managerial role in the company. That was not something Bala wanted to do. It was a fake issue; what Max really wanted was to get Bala out of the company. And as architect of the company's core technologies, Bala was reluctant to hand over his vision to someone else.

The partners began arguing over compensation. Max claimed that Bala's work did not justify a million-dollar salary, while Bala countered that developing technology was as important as Max's management skills. Then, without notice, Max unilaterally cut Bala's annual salary to $300,000, while not reducing his own salary. On top of that, when Argo moved to new corporate offices in 2006, Bala was no longer housed in the executive suite; he was relegated to an office on the lower floor without adequate secretarial and support staff. When new business cards were ordered, Bala's card was printed without a job title.

Over the next two years, Bala and Max continued to argue about salary, dividends and Bala's responsibilities going forward. During this period Max was crafting a plan to debase and impugn Bala's integrity, which would make it difficult for him to function in the company. Bala hired outside counsel to advise him on the valuation of his shares. The two managed to agree on the issuance of a dividend of $250,000—payable to them in proportion to their ownership—but otherwise the negotiations were unsuccessful. They never agreed on other issues, particularly the price Max would pay for Bala's shares.

At that point, Bala's financial adviser at Lehmann Brothers recommended that he seek legal counsel to protect his interests, and shortly thereafter, my law firm was retained. For several months, we continued to look for alternative solutions, from issuing a substantial dividend to retaining an investment banker to advise the partners on the possible sale of Argo.

At the end of 2007, frustrated by the roadblocks Max set up, Bala decided to file a lawsuit against him. The purpose of our legal action was to force Max to distribute forty-seven percent of Argo's accumulated capital as dividends, and then to value the company separately and pay Bala forty-seven percent of its value. Max would have none of that; the negotiations went nowhere. Finally, with great reluctance, Bala commenced with the suit.

During the lawsuit's discovery process over the next several years, it was revealed that what we thought was true was, in fact, true: Max had been secretly planning to buy out Bala's minority stake in Argo—with Bala's own money. The plan was elegantly hatched, with steps taken to marginalize

Bala's involvement in the company. Bala was blocked from attending numerous meetings and had no understanding of what was going on behind his back. Of the $252 million in the company's treasury, Bala believed he was entitled to over $140 million, since he had paid his share of the taxes on it. That, however, was not in Max's plan. He wanted to accumulate enough capital to buy Bala's shares by using these funds, forty-seven percent of which would ordinarily have been distributed to Bala as dividends.

The case was tried before a jury, asserting claims of shareholder oppression, "malicious suppression of dividends," fraud and other derivative claims. After six intense weeks of trial, the jury found for Bala on almost all counts and awarded damages and attorney's fees. Most significantly, the court ordered an immediate dividend in the amount of $85 million—$20 million *more* than was requested by the jury. The jury also found that Martin dominated the board of directors of Argo, resulting in conduct that was oppressive to Bala's rights as a minority shareholder, including the issuance of dividends to him.

After the verdict was rendered, I that felt we had dodged a bullet. But I also sensed the case was not over. During the trial, the counsel for Max wanted to me to know that I was in Texas, not New York, and that "things are different in Texas." I wondered what that statement might foretell about events in the future. Having spent little time in the South, I was a bit naïve about the "good old boys" network.

In his summation before the jury, Max's lawyer said that the dispute between his client and Bala could have been resolved amicably and faster but, "*Oh, no*, Bala had to go to New York instead and get himself a New York lawyer by the name of Tony Curto." Here I was, an Italian lawyer from New York with an Indian client and a Jewish trial lawyer as co-counsel. The case was a significant victory for us, but whenever such a victory occurs, you can be sure it will be appealed.

And it was.

In a stunning reversal, the Dallas Court of Appeals rejected the lower court decision in its entirety. The three-judge panel found that Max's actions did not constitute shareholder oppression and that the evidence supporting the claim of malicious suppression of dividends was not *legally* sufficient.

The court's reasoning was based on three propositions, none of which had anything to do with the actual adequacy of the evidence. The implied conclusion of the Court of Appeals was that, so long as the money was still in the company, the minority shareholder had not been harmed, or at least the majority and minority shared the same proportional benefits and disadvantages of that situation. That conclusion defied common sense. When money was to be left in the company, Max had full control, Bala had none. The suppression of Bala's dividends was involuntary; the suppression of Max's dividends was completely voluntary, subject to his control.

In rendering its decision, the Court of Appeals applied a new analysis from another shareholder case recently decided in Texas Supreme Court that distinguished the "general or specific reasonable expectations" of minority shareholders. Commenting on the case, the Fryar Law Firm, a Houston-based firm specializing in shareholder oppression, said that the decision reached in the Texas Supreme Court case was "a real and regrettable injustice." A review of the same case in the Yale Law School's *Law Journal Forum* called the court's opinion, which dealt with similar issues of law and facts as in Bala's case, astonishing. In addition, one legal commentator in Texas held that a decision of this nature gutted the cause of action for shareholder oppression cases in Texas.

It was just one in a series of anti-plaintive rulings recently handed down by the Texas Supreme Court that presented the narrowest interpretation of shareholder oppression remedies ever expressed in any judicial opinion. In his essay, the commentator added that the Texas Supreme Court had adopted a cramped and formalistic reading of the shareholder oppression statute, resulting in bad law and bad policy. These opinions provide a pretty good summary of how our legal team viewed the matter.

Since that time, the law on shareholder oppression in Texas has changed, but our day in court is long over. Bala should've had both a legal victory and a moral victory; he only got one. Usually, our legal system encourages fair play and provides favorable solutions. Yet no matter how good a case is, there is always a chance of losing. Bala knew that risk and took his chances, because in his heart he knew his cause was just. He also believed that the potential benefit of his claim, receiving millions of dollars in dividends, outweighed the risk of losing, in which case he would still have owned forty-seven percent of the company.

In hindsight, however—especially after losing a long and draining case—the question remains: Was Bala right in bringing the lawsuit, or should he have been more patient and waited for time to solve the problem?

Well, consider the situation Bala found himself in. He was a founding partner of a successful company who was relegated to having little authority over key matters; given inferior offices far away from the executive wing; and forced to take a humiliating reduction in salary. All this represented an immense attack on Bala's pride, making it impossible for him to continue working at Argo. So, yes, not only was the decision to sue justified, it was compelled.

The jury unanimously agreed that Bala was treated disgracefully by Max, which is why they found so heavily in Bala's favor. But lawsuits do not always end up in fair settlements, and more often than not, those in the right receive only a portion of what they are entitled to, while those in the wrong pay less than they should.

Ultimately, Bala sold his stock in Argo for many millions of dollars, but far less than what he should have received had the appeals court rendered a just opinion. Still, like a true entrepreneur, Bala moved on. He is now involved in multiple new projects, the most interesting of which is a private wealth management company he founded, AllocateRite, which utilizes algorithms to guide investors in the selection of securities and market timing of stock transactions. So far, the results of this recently formed company have been impressive; its investment theories have proven to be good strategies to increase clients' wealth and protect their portfolios.

Bala's only regret is that the company he co-founded is no longer his daily concern. He fathered all of Argos's technology and saw his company expand to house hundreds of employees, having a lasting impact on the banking sector nationwide. If he had had his wishes, Balkrishna Shagrithaya would still be there, developing new programs and forging into new service technologies, working with his old partner, Max Martin.

13

John Zoltak

*A wholly improbable entrepreneur who built a
visionary tech company while coping with the
challenges of bipolar disorder*

Born in 1939 in Hazelton, Pennsylvania, John "Jack" L.
Zoltak was raised in the heart of coal country. During
his teenage years, Jack attended a local mining and mechanical school and secured a job as an electrician's apprentice.
There he learned to install and maintain electrical grid systems that were essential to the operation of coal mines. After
graduating from the institute, later known as MMI Preparatory School, he completed his B.S. degree in electrical engineering and embarked on a career in avionics, the electronic
systems used in aircraft.

Jack was largely self-taught, and because the engineering
sciences came to him naturally, he excelled at his jobs. He
eventually became a highly successful entrepreneur, despite
suffering from bipolar disorder, a condition characterized by

mood swings from depression to euphoria. When Jack was young, the swings were minimal, but as he grew older they became more severe. In my relationship with Jack, I faced challenges I had never faced before as a businessman or as an attorney—and learned lessons about the lives of brilliant entrepreneurs like Jack Zoltak.

I first heard of Jack through one of my clients, Lee Pecchio, in 1979. Lee was a builder who constructed federal government housing in New York City—a wonderful man, with keen judgment and a thoughtful nature. While traveling to the city one day, Lee complained of a pain above his eye. It sounded to me as if it might be sinus condition, but I suggested that he see a doctor. The next day, Lee went to an ear, nose and throat specialist, and a series of tests determined that he had a malignant tumor on his brain.

The news was devastating to his family and friends, especially to his wife, Margaret, who had three young boys to raise and was now confronted with the daunting prospect of running the construction company and completing several U.S. Housing and Urban Development projects already underway. Any default under the terms of the contracts would have bankrupted the company, and, worse, would have bankrupted the family. Since this was a federal job, a surety bond was required, which, in effect, meant that the contracts were personally guaranteed by Lee and his wife. Materials had to be purchased, payroll met and work schedules carried out to complete the work. Margaret, without any prior experience, took on these tasks, all the while caring for a sick husband and raising her boys. A formidable job!

The Pecchio and Zoltak families were close friends, and during this period, the Zoltaks were immeasurably supportive of Margaret and her family. In the course of Lee's illness, Margaret often told me of the Zoltaks' many acts of kindness. Just before Lee's death, I ran into Jack in town and thanked him for all his support to the Pecchio family. I mentioned that if he ever needed a favor, he could call on me. Jack, with his laser-like focus, immediately told me that he needed a four-million-dollar loan to grow his undercapitalized business. Without hesitation, he asked, "Can you help?" After the shock of his request wore off, I told him I would try.

Jack had begun his career as an engineer at North American Aviation and then moved to the Harris Corporation, where he helped develop the first completely computerized avionic test system used on aircraft carriers at sea. In 1969, he founded Support Systems Associates, Inc., which delivered a broad spectrum of sophisticated technology services and products, mainly to the U.S. Air Force and Army. SSAI provided aircraft modification management systems, hardware and software designs, program management support and other essential services to help the military keep its equipment functioning. Jack stationed engineers and technicians at various military bases around the country and the world so he could respond quickly when needed. Now the company needed a loan to hire additional personnel to meet the provisions of government contracts Jack had just won.

My college roommate and close friend when I was a student at Rutgers was Richard "Dick" L. Heins, who had since risen to senior vice president at Chase Manhattan Bank, in charge of all financing deals on the East Coast. I introduced to him Jack. Dick thought SSAI had a great future and quickly approved the loan. (The relationship with Chase would continue for several years, during which time SSAI grew significantly.)

Several weeks later, after the loan was approved, I received a call from Jack, ostensibly thanking me for the introduction. I said that I was glad to help, and again expressed my appreciation for his aiding the Pecchio family in their time of dire need. After a few pleasantries, Jack said, "I would like you to run my company and become its president." I reminded Jack that I was practicing law full time and I loved it. He said he already knew that. He wanted me to continue with my practice while running his company. And I could take my staff with me.

Jack put a proposed financial package in front of me that would have doubled my income. He said he would put the deal in writing, and knowing that he had the financial resources, I had little doubt that he would make good on his promise. His goal, he said, was to be relieved of the day-to-day work because he wanted to concentrate on a "big idea"; he was certain that I was the missing piece he needed to carry out his plan. "Don't make up your mind until you meet with me," he said. So I made a date with him the following week at his home on Northport Bay on Long Island, a few houses from the Yacht Club.

It was 11:00 in the morning when I arrived at Jack's beautiful brick colonial house. As he had directed me in our telephone conversation, I went to the side entrance that led to his office. As I approached, I noticed he had a surveillance camera, so when I rang the doorbell, I was not surprised that he greeted me by name through the intercom. He was watching me. In the early 1980s this was pretty sophisticated technology, although perhaps not for a government vendor like Jack, working on secret military projects. Still, it suggested a hint of paranoia.

As I entered his study, which had a magnificent view of the bay, I was stunned by the orderliness of the room. Everything was in its place, papers meticulously arranged. His own physical image matched the look of his desk—neat and orderly.

Jack immediately launched into his pitch—that I was a perfect fit to manage the company and serve as a member of the board of directors. He said he needed someone like me so that he could pursue other interests. I had no idea what those interests were, so I asked him, and he described an elaborate plan to capture the power of the tides that flow in and out of shorelines in all quarters of the world. He handed me a worksheet, showing his calculations of the power that could be generated by tides and the number of megawatts of electricity that could be supplied through the use of colossal underwater paddle-wheel generators.

As Jack continued to talk, supplying me with a torrent of details, his language and gestures became more and more grandiose. At first, I felt overwhelmed by his brilliance. But as he went on, I became uneasy. There are times when you hear people talk and you ask yourself, "Am I crazy…. or is *he* crazy?" The more he talked, the more I was convinced he was suffering from some form of mental illness.

On the way out of the house, Jack's wife, Margi, accompanied me, and when Jack's back was turned, she whispered, "Help me." I nodded. I said I would do what I could. Obviously, something was wrong. And she knew it.

Over the next few days, I had several separate phone conversations with Jack and Margi. With him, I discussed the potential business arrangement with me and compensation. With her, I discussed Jack's mental problems and possible solutions. We needed to find a way to arrange for a psychological examination with a qualified expert, but Margi told me that Jack had previously resisted any such exam.

I was playing for time. I needed a plan that could get Jack examined by a qualified psychologist to support an involuntary commitment to a hospital. I didn't know whether the problem was physiological or psychological, but I knew I had to get Jack examined.

Then I hit upon an idea. There was a well-known local psychologist, Doug Woods, whom Jack and I knew as members of the local yacht club. In one of our conversations I suggested to Jack that we should submit ourselves to Dr. Woods for an evaluation that would assess our personalities, and more important, our compatibility, before I took over management of his company. This would be a good way to ensure our chances for success. After some discussion, he agreed. We made an appointment to meet at Jack's house the following week at 8:00 in the evening.

As Doug and I approached Jack's home at the appointed time, I heard the roar of an engine. When I rang the doorbell, Margi answered, and I heard the engine roar again, this time more clearly from the bay side of the house. The noise came from a helicopter taking off from the back lawn. I turned to Doug and said, "Guess who's in the helicopter?" It was a scene right out of a James Bond movie. As we were entering the house, setting our trap, Jack was making his timely escape out the back; he was on to our trick. Margi revealed that he had been planning some sort of escape since I suggested psychological testing.

This was the beginning of an amazing chase that lasted several weeks.

As I began devising another scheme to bring Jack in for medical treatment, I focused on the fact that he was an enthusiastic fan of the New York Islanders, Long Island's pro hockey team, who were playing in the finals of the Stanley Cup championship. He loved the sport and had season tickets, as did I. Since the Islanders were in the playoffs for the first time in their relatively short history, I knew that he would be attending the series. Over the course of several Islander games, Jack would send me messages through intermediaries, taunting me: Go ahead, try and catch me. I knew he was at the games, but I couldn't figure out where he was. I found out later that he was wearing disguises and constantly moving around. It was a cat-and-mouse game—and he was winning.

During this period, I was frequently in touch with Margi, who told me that Jack would occasionally come home to pick up clean clothes, say hello and goodbye. She also told me that Jack had a shotgun with him. Jack was brought up in rural Pennsylvania, where hunting and fishing were part of his life. I told her that if he came during the day, she should call me at the office, and I would try to confront him. At the time, I was the Northport Village Justice and knew everyone on the local police force.

One afternoon, I got the call from Margi: Jack was back. I alerted the town police that I might need some assistance. Shortly thereafter, I was walking on Main Street when I spied Jack on the corner. He saw me, too. As he started to run, I gave chase, sprinting down the street with the police right behind me. He was heading for the water, and I was afraid he had a boat stashed at the dock, ready to make his watery getaway. Right before he got to the dock, I caught up and tackled him. I was on top of Jack; the police were on top of me. With his face pressed against the ground, he looked up at me forlornly and said, "I thought you were my friend."

To this day I regret that I had to bring Jack to the ground, and of course, I felt terrible about his disappointment in me. He was a captain of industry and a prominent citizen of the community. But we saw no alternative but to capture him the way we did. His behavior had become so erratic that we were concerned about what actions he might take that could destroy his highly successful company. Jack was working on many secret government programs that required top clearance. If he lost that security status, he could also have lost his contracts, and SSAI would have spun out of control in relatively short order.

After several weeks of medical treatment with lithium, Jack was released from the hospital. He appeared to be quite normal. He invited me to be on his board of directors and I said that I would attend meetings, but I didn't want to join the board just yet, since I didn't know enough about the company. After attending several meetings, I still felt uncomfortable with the board members. I thought they had been taking advantage of Jack; I wasn't sure who could be trusted—and who could not.

Several months went by, and I started to get a better handle on the company. But as I developed a plan to help Jack get everything back on track, I noticed his behavior slipping back into a pattern of actions reminiscent of the first time I met him. It was upsetting to see Jack surrounded by sycophants who, because they were well paid, didn't want to rock the boat. Jack reminded me of Howard Hughes, and people like him—often isolated and well protected, while their medical condition goes ignored and untreated.

Then, at a board meeting, I detected an increase in Jack's bizarre behavior. Because he was chairing the meeting, I waited until afterward to confront him. "If I find you slipping back into your manic behavior, do you want me to intervene?" I asked. He looked at me and said, "No." Furthermore, he said, my tackling him on Main Street was a humiliating experience.

Thinking over my involvement with Jack, as a neighbor and friend, I realized I had done all I could do. I left him alone. But a few weeks later I heard that he had gone to Saudi Arabia, where he attempted to make a large purchase of precious gems—part of a scheme to corner the market on a particular type of stone. His aberrant behavior came to the attention of the American ambassador, who arranged for his detainment and sent him home, where he was again hospitalized and treated.

I had learned some time ago that there are situations where you can be of help, and there are situations you should avoid. This was one of the latter, so I stepped out. Over the next several years, I occasionally met Jack around town. He was cordial, but under his calm demeanor I could sense his anger. He made it clear without words that he did not look with favor on my intervention, nor did he appreciate what I done to help preserve his company and his family.

The business that Jack had created was ahead of its time. He foresaw the strategic need to place electronic support facilities on military bases, thereby reducing the time and cost of keeping equipment and machines in service. His company always had expert staff on site who could repair and replace sophisticated equipment with a minimum of turnaround time. Jack's concept had a lot of complicated parts, but his vision was simple and clear. He saw his company's value grow to more than ten million dollars.

Despite Jack's mental disorder, many of his former employees remembered him fondly after his recent death: He was a leader who not only built a cutting-edge company but had a major impact on their lives.

A veteran from Virginia Beach recalled that Jack was his first employer after he completed his naval career. Jack made his transition "seamless, by providing knowledge, trust and empowerment," he said, "and I soon realized that I was associated with the epitome of the American dream."

Another former employee, from Walton Beach, Florida, noted that Jack "was a great mentor to me when I first retired from the military. He pushed me to finish my education, something that no one in the military was able to do. His tenacity was his true strength and as a result, my family is much stronger today."

Still other SSAI employees marveled at Jack's uncanny ability to analyze complex situations and come up with the right, and often simple, solutions. They saluted him as a "leader who could be counted on to make tough decisions and press forward."

In considering Jack among the array of entrepreneurs I knew over the years, I've come to recognize some common entrepreneurial traits: They have big ideas and a lot of energy. They have the will never to give up, to see a project through, even when confronted by unexpected challenges that require a major change in their plans. When these entrepreneurs are confronted by a problem that is absolutely not solvable, they come up with a new idea and pursue it with the same vigor as the old one, provided that this grand new idea will also bring the company to a higher level of performance.

In Jack's case, the new ideas mostly came from his unique brain chemistry. When Jack was in his manic phase, thoughts would explode from his mind, and he pursued them with vigor and optimism. He reminded me of other creative individuals who are said to have suffered from bipolar disorder, who nevertheless achieved fame and success in their lifetimes: an impressive list of artists, from Ernest Hemingway, Vincent Van Gogh, Frank Sinatra and Robert Schumann to contemporary celebrities like Francis Ford Coppola, Richard Dreyfuss, Lou Reed, Margot Kidder, Kanye West and dozens more.

When Jack was taking his medicine, he exuded a normal amount of energy and would settle into a routine of simply managing his business. But his entrepreneurial genius, like the burst of brilliance from great artists—well, that was created by a mind on fire!

14

Harrison Salisbury

A prize-winning New York Times correspondent who broke journalistic tradition with the nation's first op-ed page, while serving as a wise mentor to the next generation—including me

In the early 1960s I met a man who would change my professional life.

I was fresh out of law school, tackling my first job as a sixty-dollar-a-week law clerk at a boutique Manhattan law firm while studying for the bar exam. Suddenly, I found myself surrounded by celebrated writers, journalists, artists, actors, producers and business moguls. The firm's glittering list of clients ranged from famed financier and philanthropist Bernard Baruch to a strong-willed Swedish film star who became known as Greta Garbo.

It also included a prize-winning reporter for *The New York Times*, Harrison E. Salisbury.

Harrison Salisbury had recently returned to the United States from the Soviet Union, where he had been *Times* bureau chief of the Moscow desk from 1949 to 1954. At a social event one evening, Harrison and I were seated next to each other. After a few hours of pleasant conversation, he suddenly said to me, "I don't have a lawyer. You're my lawyer."

Harrison became my client in 1960, and over the years I advised him on multiple projects, including many books. He was at the center of an extraordinary network of literary, media and artistic figures, introducing me to the likes of Walter Cronkite and Arthur Miller.

But Harrison would come to assume a much larger role for me: He became my close friend and mentor. It's unusual for a young lawyer to have a non-lawyer as his mentor; it is even more unusual to have a client as your mentor. Clients turn to lawyers for advice; they're generally not the ones *giving* advice to their attorneys. I had always been a tough advocate. Harrison, an intrepid correspondent, taught me how to read situations with greater objectivity, distinguishing the important battles from mere skirmishes. Most of all, he taught me how to analyze problems globally and search for answers that were "win-win" solutions. As the years went by, our relationship grew as we taught and learned from each other. These interactions with Harrison contributed enormously to my success; I count them among the best experiences of my life.

Before joining *The New York Times* in 1949, Harrison was the United Press's overseas foreign editor, which helped prepare him for the *Times* Moscow Bureau. During his tenure in Moscow he constantly battled with Soviet censors in his efforts to peek behind the Iron Curtain. Because of his persistence and journalistic intuitiveness, he uncovered story after story, several of them published as a series of articles after he returned from Moscow, which won him a Pulitzer Prize in 1955.

His broad knowledge of the Soviet Union led him to another international adventure. Identified by the dissident Russian literary community as a champion of artistic freedom, Harrison became part of a small group of Americans who put together a secret plan to publish the novels of renowned Russian writer Aleksandr Solzhenitsyn in the West. It was Harrison who brought me into this group as the attorney responsible for representing Solzhenitsyn during six years of complex and sometimes dangerous negotiations.

Harrison was an integral part of the long tradition of journalistic excellence at the *Times,* which was founded in 1851. In addition to winning a Pulitzer, Harrison twice received the George Polk Award for foreign reporting. In the 1960s he covered the civil rights movement in the southern United States, occasionally risking physical harm. His incisive reports about the "emotional dynamite of racism" in Birmingham, Alabama, provoked several libel suits, eventually dismissed by a U.S. Court of Appeals, which noted that the *Times* had "exhibited a high standard of reporting practices." Harrison directed the *Times*'s coverage of the assassination of President John F. Kennedy, remaining at his desk in the newsroom almost around the clock for days after the assassination. Later, he wrote the introduction to the Warren Commission Report, the 888-page compilation of all the available facts and circumstances leading to the death of the president.

He became assistant managing editor of the *Times* in 1964 and associate editor in 1970. As an editor, he never lost his zeal for dogged, in-depth reporting, and his stature gave him the freedom to roam the landscape for stories of interest. Recalling his time as a foreign correspondent, he noted that he spent much of his life "visiting difficult, impossible countries—Communist countries, for the most part."

He was very much a journalistic entrepreneur, always anticipating the needs of his customers, the American public. His product was information and analysis, identifying the questions that needed to be answered—or should have been asked—and providing answers to those questions.

In 1970 Harrison was among a handful of editors who created the iconic op-ed page for the "Gray Lady," a page of essays, columns, articles and opinion pieces that appears opposite the editorial page. Before the launch of the op-ed page, the newspaper offered a relatively small amount of space for columns and articles expressing the opinions of the publisher. The op-ed page format provided a variety of perspectives from a wide range of outside writers and thinkers, balancing the paper's news coverage. Readers were dealt the responsibility of integrating news and opinion pieces into a comprehensive understanding of current events.

As the first editor of the op-ed page, Harrison set the standard for writers around the country, initiating and instigating discussions pertinent to the fast-changing times we live in. Like most entrepreneurial ideas, it was a risk, and Harrison would later say that he initially worried the paper would soon run out of submissions. That would not be the case. In fact, the op-ed page was such a good idea that it was quickly copied by newspapers around the country, and the tradition continues to flourish today. "Everyone in the country wanted to speak out," Harrison recalled, "and we let their voices be heard."

Harrison had a remarkable instinct for putting himself in the right place at the right time—where history was being made. While filming a TV documentary in Beijing, China, in 1989, for example, he observed the bloody revolt against the Chinese government in Tiananmen Square. His prescience was almost freakish: He was the sole western journalist on the scene, and his reporting was the only objective narrative to emerge from Communist China.

Among the most significant reporting Harrison did was in North Vietnam during the winter of 1966 and 1967, which he recounted in his book, *Behind Enemy Lines—Hanoi.*

During the Christmas holiday season, I received a telephone call from Harrison in my office, asking whether all his personal affairs—his estate plan, his power of attorney and life insurance policies—were in order. I said they were. He explained that he was leaving the country on a top-level reporting mission, and while he could not talk about over the phone, I would be hearing about it soon. I was baffled; I had no idea what he was up to.

Then one day between Christmas and New Year's, I was shoveling snow off the rear deck of my home, listening to the news on the house intercom radio, when I heard that Harrison had gotten behind the lines in North Vietnam and was reporting from that country. I couldn't wait to read his dispatches, which were appearing on the front page of *The New York Times.*

A few weeks later, I received an air mail letter from Harrison. It was short but memorable—a keepsake—dated January 3, 1967:

Dear Tony:

The chief purpose of this is to let you have a letter with the Hanoi postmark and Vietnam stamp on it —they don't come around very often and who knows when I may have a chance to do this again.

I will be getting back in a little more than a week, I think. It has been a tremendously productive trip as you know although it did come at a rough time as far as home life was concerned—but I guess [his wife] Charlotte has all in hand—she is good at that.

All the best to you and a real good New Year,

As ever,
Harrison

Unbeknownst to me, Harrison had spent many months attempting to secure a visa into North Vietnam. It had been no easy task. His campaign to gain admission went on week after week, as he wrote letters to political officials, journalists, professors—anyone he could think of who might intervene on his behalf. He finally got a visa ten days before Christmas—with no advance notice—but at an auspicious time: North Vietnamese authorities were claiming that American planes had dropped bombs for the first time within the principal urban area of Hanoi.

Harrison secretly departed on an arduous air journey from Paris to Albania, then Egypt and then across Asia to Phnom Penh, Cambodia. It was not certain that he would ever get to Hanoi until the occasional, often-canceled flight from Phnom Penh actually landed.

Harrison was never quite certain why his visa was approved. Perhaps it was because it was around Christmas, a time of traditional truces during war. But perhaps there was another reason: Harrison's reputation was as an honest reporter who showed a willingness to listen and give account to stories that were out of favor with the government. At the time, he wrote in his diary:

I think my trip is supposed to convey an image of confidence, of hardihood in the face of U.S. bombing…a positive image of North Vietnam but at the same time it is designed to bring peace or a truce or talks nearer, in part by assuring the U.S. and U.S. opinion that the present policy is not winning...

Harrison wanted to interview three key leaders: Ho Chi Minh, president of North Vietnam; General Vo Nguyen Giap, the military strategist for Ho's Vietnamese Communist forces; and Premier Pham Van Dong, the working chief executive of North Vietnam. Harrison didn't think he would get interviews with all three men but hoped that he would get two out of three. He wrote a list of questions, which he hoped would stimulate interest in meeting for more extensive interviews.

As it turned out, Harrison was granted a meeting only with Premier Dong, but he was not disappointed. Dong was "a man of brilliance and considerable wit, possessing a personality which ranged through a variety of emotions," as Harrison recalled in *Behind Enemy Lines*. Their wide-ranging discussion lasted four and a half hours and mostly coincided with what Harrison was told by people at various levels of North Vietnamese society, ranging from the peasants in the streets and laborers to government workers and higher-echelon government employees. They echoed similar thoughts. As a people, the North Vietnamese were prepared for a long war that could last ten or twenty years. They were fiercely proud of their independence, not only from the colonial French and Japanese invaders from World War II but from communist Russia and China.

Vietnam's document proclaiming its independence, which Ho had written himself, opened with almost an exact quotation from the U.S. Declaration of Independence:

"All men are created equal. They are endowed by their Creator with certain inalienable rights, among these are life, liberty and the pursuit of happiness."

Although Ho was a member of the French communist party, there were numerous anti-communists in the top brackets and the North Vietnamese leadership. In fact, Ho was deftly playing the Russians and Chinese against one other, in an attempt to avoid a show of favoritism while ensuring he got the supplies they needed to fight the war.

During his stay in North Vietnam, Harrison took a number of side trips through cities and the countryside to view the damage done by American bombs that had been dropped earlier that month. He saw little evidence that there was a strategic military plan; the bombings appeared to be random and imprecise. Harrison's reporting pointed out several serious discrepancies between his observations and the pronouncements made by the U.S. government.

By the time Harrison left Hanoi, he was convinced that the North Vietnamese would not have let him into the country unless they had already decided that the time had come for an active exploration of the possibility of peaceful negotiation. As Harrison wrote in *Behind Enemy Lines,* he believed "the arguments ran strongly toward an effort at negotiation," but he also recognized the realities of Washington—that many leaders at the Pentagon and in Congress believed that the war "must be remorselessly pressed and escalated to the limit."

The principal issue driving America's involvement in this war was the widely expressed fear of the effects of the "domino theory." Top military and political strategists in the United States, including Secretary of Defense Robert McNamara, believed that America had to defend South Vietnam in order to stop the march of communism through Asia. This fear drove most of the policy decisions of the United States and was the principal misconception that Harrison believed was revealed by his investigations.

Harrison's reports, which were printed on the first page of *The New York Times,* struck a nerve in the public; people were starting to suspect that the government was not telling the whole truth about the war. The seeds of discontent were beginning to be sown, even as a majority of Americans still believed that this war had to be waged and won. Most observers of the time believe that it was Harrison Salisbury's dispatches that helped turned the tide against the Vietnam War, prompting President Lyndon Johnson's decision not to seek the presidency after his term expired.

Many historians also maintain that the time of the Vietnam War was a turning point in the history of our country, citing significant changes in the economy, culture and politics. In 1965, before our efforts to win the war intensified, the inflation rate in the country was less than one percent. Over the next five years the rate of inflation tripled, as government spending ballooned. In 1965, the total debt of the U.S. government was three-hundred-billion dollars. That amount had been climbing gradually over the prior hundred years, through two world wars and the Great Depression. Over the next ten years the debt grew by sixty percent to five hundred billion, ushering in the double-digit inflation rates of the 1970s.

Our soldiers went to war looking like Pat Boone; they returned part of the Grateful Dead generation. With their familiarity with and dependence on drugs, they merged with the Woodstock generation to become a dominant part of the culture; and so it continues to this day. You can quantify the number of deaths that have occurred through overdoses and excessive use, but you can't quantify the number of lies that have been perpetuated by the glorification of the drug culture.

From time to time, Harrison would talk to me about the impact of the Vietnam War on America. He felt that as a result of the war, the populace had become suspicious of its leaders and cynical about their government's pronouncements. As the size of government expanded and the influence of the individual diminished, this public distrust grew. Idealism and patriotism waned, replaced by self-indulgence and a me-too philosophy. Harrison addressed some of these concerns in his book *The Shook-Up Generation*. The young people he described had become mature adults, entering positions of leadership—or rather, non-leadership, having abdicated their rightful place as the guiding hands of the next generation. Today, government institutions that had previously been under public scrutiny are now largely controlled by political operatives and bureaucratic deep staters.

The damage to our culture that emerged from the Vietnam era has been incalculable, reverberating through our beliefs in God, education and family. Sex and violence as depicted by the entertainment industry, with cruel and often superficial but titillating action, have displaced classic themes of human challenges and struggles for survival. Everything seems to have turned commercial. "What's in it for me?" is the current aspiration of our time. In contrast, John F. Kennedy's intonation: "Ask not what your country can do for you—ask what you can you do for your country" is barely remembered.

In assessing Harrison's overall accomplishments, it is easy to see why he achieved such prominence. Because of his remarkable reporting and writing skills, he could pursue stories that compelled retelling, writing twenty-nine books over the course of his career. Two that stand out for me are *The 900 Days: The Siege of Leningrad*, his bestseller about how the Russian city withstood a protracted Nazi siege during World War II, and *The Long March*, the untold story of chairman Mao's revolutionary ascendance to the premiership of China.

For me, of course, Harrison was much more than a writer and a reporter. He was an energetic pioneer who caused change. Whether writing for the intellectual readership of the *Times* or for the wider public, he staked out a territory where truth and morality dominated. He brought this approach into the newsroom itself, where his door was always open and his counsel available to young reporters. Many of these hand-picked young journalists showed promise but needed guidance to bring them into the big leagues. He always had time for them; he read their work and critiqued their articles, challenged them to become premier journalists, not just good writers. It was a sweat-intensive enterprise that required these newbies to jump into life with both feet, get out into the field and cultivate informed sources who knew what was going on. He wanted them to understand not only what was on the surface, but also what was happening behind the scenes, and to be able to anticipate future events and trends. I had a front row seat to all these goings-on, and in many instances, I took part in these memorable events and stories.

Still, *The New York Times* was not an easy place to work. These were extraordinary, driven people; the competition was keen and so was the political infighting. Even the social activity at cocktail parties was intense, with conversations misunderstood and misinterpreted, sometimes deliberately. The fierce competitiveness of the overall media environment demanded accuracy, speed and liveliness. Management required constant improvement, which, not surprisingly, resulted in numerous purges, where people were either advanced or replaced.

This addictive and competitive atmosphere was a challenge to navigate—and this is where I learned the most from Harrison. Because he was emotionally healthy, having beaten alcoholism in his early years, Harrison understood the ego drives of those around him and did not take personally many of the unintentional transgressions afflicted by co-workers upon one another. He knew how to negotiate around those egos without losing his core beliefs, maintaining the objective air of an academic.

Harrison knew the battles that had to be fought and won, and he knew how to avoid the sucker fights that had no value, leaving you only diminished. He rose through the ranks as his colleagues became trusting and respectful of his nature; they could see his talents in a less threatening way.

Harrison was an indefatigable writer till the end. His last book, *Heroes of My Time*, a set of recollections of remarkable people he had met over his lifetime, was published just before he died in 1993. In a review of the book, Michael Janeway, the dean of the Medill School of Journalism, remembered Harrison as a "daring, savvy old soldier of the press who'd seen it all." At a time when journalism was "short of institutional elders," Janeway noted, Harrison was "a living monument to the fine perversity of the reporter in the field who deals in grit, risks life and limb and tilts toward unorthodoxy."

In Harrison's will, I was designated as his literary trustee, charged with managing and advancing his lifetime of written works. Since my partial retirement I have transferred these rights to his two sons for administration, knowing that they are in good hands. They are a trove of far-flung reports and opinions that will give insight into Harrison's times and travels for many years to come.

15

Chester Broman

*A man of the earth who pioneered the science of
environmentally sustainable landfills—"dumps"
no more!*

Chester Broman has spent all his life in the dirt. He has
dug dirt, moved dirt, sold dirt—he has even sold the
hole from which the dirt came.

Chester constructed and supervised the operation of one
of the largest landfills in the northeast. It would become the
national model for operators who were required to meet the
rigorous standards of the New York State Department of
Environmental Conservation and the federal Environmental Protection Agency.

Years ago, landfills were called "dumps." The word fit the
image: a place where all forms of refuse were indiscriminately
piled high. Today, dumps are classified by the type of refuse
they accept. Chester's landfill was permitted by state and
federal regulatory agencies for the collection of construction

and demolition waste," known as C&D. His landfill was often the site where new DEC officials were brought for observation of and instruction in new procedures that could be adapted for wide implementation. Chester's lifelong contribution to the fight against pollution makes him one of the most civic-minded entrepreneurs I've ever represented.

In earlier times, construction debris was often discarded in empty lots and vacant property. As our population increased, our waste also increased, and so did the contamination of our land, water and air. Unregulated dumping has brought health issues to our communities, where waste was often transported by rivers, other times by plumes from contaminated underground aquifers, or simply by the spreading of refuse on virgin land.

From peak to trough, the debris in Chester's landfill created a pile the height of about two-hundred feet—essentially a twenty-story building. All the C&D material was properly assayed and sealed off from the water table to prevent its migration, especially its chemical components, into the groundwater. Collection wells also had to be built into the cells to provide for the gathering of gases and contaminated water. It was an elaborate, labyrinthian structure of interconnecting tubes, barriers and pipes for the collection of tainted media. Constructing such a landfill was a formidable undertaking, supervised by Chester and his staff, that required strict compliance with technical environmental standards and regulations.

Chester left college after one semester, but he had an intuitive intelligence that helped him gain a quick grasp of pollution problems. Every year, government regulators would issue new directives that often contradicted prior directives. Chester was one of those entrepreneurs who abided not only by the letter of the law but also by the spirit of the law. This made it possible for him to stay ahead of present-day requirements and to anticipate likely changes that would eventually be needed to maintain a landfill free of contamination.

Chester was a simple, modest man in both words and actions. He was self-effacing, hardly ever exhibiting any visible ego, considering his exemplary achievements. His regular business dealings were always direct and honest; his word, which he gave after careful consideration, was always honored. In the forty-five years that I represented Chester he never sued, nor has he been sued, by anyone. His approach has always been to go from problems to solutions, with logic and ease.

Chester first assumed operational responsibilities of a 285-acre landfill, located in Suffolk County, Long Island, after years in the trucking business. When the landfill opened, the surrounding area was sparsely settled. As Long Island grew, so did the problems handling the region's waste and its storage. It didn't take long for the Island's exploding suburban sprawl to encircle Chester's landfill, raising community concerns about health and safety. Such concerns attracted intense political and governmental scrutiny, even though these homeowners knew when they purchased their homes that they were living next to a landfill.

Balancing public health with the requirements of facilities that took in construction debris meant that Chester had to be plugged in to latest science for the remediation of contaminants, as well as staying on top of the government's ongoing requirements for monitoring ground, air and water data. These were the challenges presented by constantly decaying organic and inorganic materials.

On top of that, there was the charged political relationship with local community governing authorities. There was zero tolerance for noise, odor or contamination of any kind. Even if the landfill was established long before the surrounding residential communities were built and it met strict government standards.

Chester Broman knew from the beginning that it was imperative to establish a model operation, free from legitimate community and governmental complaints. This was not an easy task, however, because technology and environmental regulations kept evolving at a fast pace, with new standards requiring immediate implementation. In many respects, Chester's landfill was the laboratory for the testing of new ideas, transitioning between old and new standards, while still enabling the business to continue making a profit. Chester employed numerous experts to interpret the laws and implement the technological advances necessary not only to meet the current standards but also to provide flexibility to meet future regulations that were sure to come.

Time and decay are nature's friends—and they give a helping hand to landfills. During the fifty years between the burial of debris and the full decomposition of this debris underground, all waste has to be securely contained. Easier said than done. Landfill facilities are subject to all weather and environmental conditions, including rain, heat, cold and "compaction," the compressing of debris so it takes up less space. Containment is made more difficult when rain falls over the compacted field, resulting in a slurry of waste called leachate. Latest technology and regulations require the elaborate use of barriers, liners, collection ports and air monitors to eliminate the migration of the waste and ultimately to provide for its collection and disposal. The way leachate and methane gas are neutralized determines the success or failure of a landfill.

In the early years of environmental regulation, federal and New York State agencies permitted gases to be expelled into the atmosphere through exhaust ports. Later, the law required tall stacks be used to exhaust the gases into higher dispersal winds. When this proved to be inefficient, landfill operators were permitted to burn the methane gases, producing flames that could be seen at night coming from these high stacks. Ultimately, the U.S. Clean Air Act prohibited the burning of these gases because of the excessive emission of hydrocarbons into the atmosphere.

Landfill operators had to constantly scramble to keep in compliance. Practices that were once permitted were now prohibited. Operators had to find ways to quickly comply or face substantial fines. Since sheetrock, wood and metals, together with crushed concrete, all emit contaminated liquids and gases when rained on, their effluent had to be collected, contained and remediated with new processes and technologies.

In order to ensure zero emissions, Chester investigated technology from around the world. The project was an extraordinary undertaking, taking years in development and tens of millions of dollars. Ultimately, Chester built an immense facility, roughly the size of a big box store, which collected this tainted waste slurry and processed it into potable water and commercial sulfur, a feat not unlike biblical transfiguration. To accomplish this miracle, Chester employed the services of thousands of workers—only five of them human, the balance millions of nonhuman workers called microbes that worked day and night to transform this slurry into harmless byproducts. Chester would often joke that of all the workers he ever employed, these were the best. They worked overtime, never complained and did a first-rate job!

The resulting state-of-the-art facility was the first iteration of new technology employed in the United States to solve the problem of landfill waste, and it was regarded as a true technological advancement. Its success can be validated by the zero level of legitimate complaints registered by the neighbors and regulatory agencies over the last ten years. And a good part of this success can also to be attributed to Chester's top-level managers, highly motivated people carefully selected by Chester, all of whom have been with him for many years and became highly regarded professionals during the term of their employment.

Chester is the quintessential small business entrepreneur, capable of wearing many hats while pursuing multiple goals. One of his other interests has been the breeding and training of Thoroughbred racehorses. Every year there are about ten thousand horses bred for racing in the United States, but only about twenty make it into the Kentucky Derby. It is a long shot, to be sure, but Chester, with the same kind of attention to detail he employs in his landfill business, set out to produce a Derby participant, and hopefully a Derby winner, each year. Chester's horse, Friends Lake, didn't win the Derby, but he ran the race, and Chester has had scores of horses that did win him major championships, such as the Florida Derby and the Breeders' Cup.

Through his involvement with horse racing and his service on the board of the New York Racing Association, Chester became aware of the difficulty finding suitable facilities for retired racehorses, sparing them from the glue factory or the dog food dispensary. In response, Chester has been pursuing a charitable foundation for the care of retired horses in Chesterton, New York that can handle over seventy horses at a time.

So what kind of an entrepreneur was Chester? A dreamer? No. A communicator? No. Was he bound to a set philosophy? No.

He was just pragmatic. If he had a problem, he would find a solution. He was up at five in the morning and on the job by six every day. He wanted to know everything that was happening in the field and in the office. I don't think I saw him in a suit more than four times—and that was usually a tuxedo.

Chester trusted his people and listened to them with great patience. I often felt that he had made up his mind about things in advance, but he was willing to listen to the opinions of others. While his politeness may have passed for sensitivity, I believe he had little interest in people's feelings. But he was good-hearted and ethical, and he felt that if he did the right thing, people's feelings would not be a problem; that was his goal. Chester and his wife, Mary, raised three children, and the family has made numerous charitable gifts to their church, which has enabled it to continue its good work.

Chester always liked being in charge. He was just as likely to do nothing—and then take a great risk, with the chance for a high reward. He was happiest when he was building something. A new plant to extract toxins from the soil and air, yes. A cutting-edge, hundred-horse stable and farm, yes. He was not interested in their aesthetics, so long as it was well constructed and fully functional and solved the problem.

A friend whom I've known for years, Congressman Tom Suozzi from New York, cites his father's favorite Italian saying: "Don't pay attention to a person's words. Watch their hands."

Chester's hands tell the story.

16

Millionaires in Bermuda Shorts

A cautionary tale of intrepid youth who crossed legal in search of the fast lane to wealth

I n the summer of 1976, I met a crew of enterprising young men who were sailing racing boats along the southeastern coast of the United States. They were an accomplished group that had sailed together many times, and as I discovered afterward, they had an adventurous entrepreneurial spirit—but they were operating on the wrong side of the law. It was a disconcerting experience, but it reaffirmed the moral compass of my legal career. While I remained committed to helping aspiring entrepreneurs achieve their goals, there were lines that I would not cross—even when there was the possibility of great financial reward.

The story actually began a year earlier, in 1975. I had built and skippered a boat, the *Sting Act II*, which won the Midget Ocean Racing Club (MORC) world championship

185

on Block Island Sound off the shores of Rhode Island. Now, with a new version of my boat called *Stung Over*, I wanted to repeat the previous year's performance, this time in the championship regatta on the Chesapeake Bay, in Maryland. Our team had spent the entire winter reconfiguring the design of our boat to make it faster. We were pleased with the results, and we felt confident going into the racing season.

But it quickly became apparent that our new boat did not perform as we expected. The fleet of boats we would be racing against had improved over the course of the winter. Some of the new boats were exploring different design philosophies to correct their shortcomings and improve speed.

At the time, most boats were displacement sailing boats, meaning that as they went through the water, they had to displace their weight in water. If a boat weighed, say, a ton, it would have to displace a ton of water, so its speed would be limited by the laws of physics. The new boats, however, were designed so they were able to plane, to be lifted out of the water. They were no longer limited by the physics of displacement and thus were able to reach greater speeds. Winning was going to be much harder. That's usually the case, but this year the advancements in design and sailing techniques were unprecedented.

I had sailed Chesapeake Bay only a few times before, once with Ted Turner on his boat, *Tenacious*, and on prior occasions in the Chesapeake Fall Series, a well-known regatta that included hundreds of boats of different classes. This time around, I decided I would leave my boat home and try racing aboard one of the newer, non-displacement boats.

Since I was the commodore of MORC and had won the championship regatta before, I had the privilege of participating in the '76 regatta on other boats. After some study, I picked a boat I thought had a good chance of winning it all. When I asked the captain whether there was room on his boat, he offered me the navigation job. I took it.

My new boat had a highly qualified crew. They had sailed together many times; a few were professional sailors with America's Cup experience. I had sailed with some of them, too, or knew them by reputation. For the most part, however, these guys were strangers to me, although they were a friendly group.

An international regatta like this one is usually raced over a period of a week, during which five races or more are held, covering different distances, the longest one probably a hundred-plus miles. Some of the seven-man crew slept aboard the boat; most slept ashore. No matter where we slept, it's no surprise that we became fairly close, after spending over a hundred hours sailing together. There was plenty of time to get to know one another and share stories—and this group had plenty of them.

Much of my time with the crew was spent discussing my favorite topics over cold beers: taxation, investing and business issues. One crew member seemed to take a particular interest in hearing about my career, and at the end of the week, he explained that he was the first mate on a seventy-three-foot yawl whose owner, he believed, would want to hear my thoughts on taxation and investments. He said he would be up north with the boat and its owner in the late fall; perhaps we could meet at the Derecktor Shipyard in Mamaroneck. I told him to let me know when he would be there, and if I could arrange my schedule, we could meet at the shipyard.

From time to time, I noticed that a number of the young crew would stay in the front cabin, or forecastle, for long periods of time. Occasionally, I would smell something burning, although I wasn't sure what it was. Overall, though,

I had a great experience with these professionals and their crew, who handled the boat like a well-choreographed dance team. We won the regatta handily.

Several months later, in early November, I received a follow-up call from my curious young sailing buddy, inviting me to meet him and the owner of his boat at the Derecktor Shipyard. Frankly, I was surprised, because the owner of a multimillion-dollar yacht doesn't usually take tax and investment advice from his teenage first mate. I was familiar with the shipyard. It was a well-known facility, founded by "Old Man" Bob Derecktor, whose company had a reputation for constructing and maintaining mega-yachts. I had been there several times before, when America's Cup boats were being either built or docked there.

On the day of the meeting, I walked down the gangplank to the floating docks, looking for my friend's double-masted yacht. It wasn't hard to find; the main mast must have been at least one hundred feet high, and most of the other boats had already been taken out the water for winter storage.

It was a magnificent boat, well-appointed and carefully maintained. It had all the bells and whistles. When I rapped on the side of the hull, my friend immediately appeared from below and invited me aboard. The main salon was spacious and paneled in varnished mahogany. There, I was introduced to a young man who was only identified by his first name. He seemed too young to be the owner, but anyway, we started to talk. I soon got the feeling that I didn't have the whole story about my friend, or whoever was the owner of this yacht. I began describing my firm and my credentials, but the conversation was awkward.

Suddenly, my friend stood up and walked into the middle of the cabin. He removed two floorboards, reached down and drew two gigantic plastic bags from the bilge. He placed the bags in front of me, opened them and showed me their contents: bundles of cash, who knew how much. Now I realized why I was there. They wanted me to take this cash and "invest" it for them. There was a term for what they were asking me to do: It was called money laundering, I said, and it was a crime. Then I had another "aha!" moment. That funny smell I remembered coming from the fore-peak of the boat? The crew members were smoking pot.

Obviously, the financial return on their marijuana business was impressive, and the pay they offered me was substantial. I delivered a long explanation as to why I wouldn't undertake the job. I gave them moral and practical reasons and counseled them to take their spoils, go straight and live a good and honest life. In every person's life there are moments when important decisions have to be made, and this was a crisis moment for me. I was never suckered by money, perhaps because I had what I needed, but more likely because I had dreams that money could not buy. I knew which way I was going, but I hoped I could use this occasion to instruct, to provide some guidance for them, because I had a premonition that it was going to turn out badly. Which it did.

On the way out, I said to my friend, "Sorry I can't help you, but if you ever get into a problem and need my legal help, I would be happy to assist you."

I thought this would be the end of the story, but no. The following year, on a Friday evening before Christmas, I received a call from my sailing friend. He was in a Virginia jail. He had one phone call to make and he made it to me.

He explained that he and his sailing buddies from the Chesapeake regatta had bought a barge, towed it to the Bahamas, filled it with five tons of marijuana and brought it to the East Coast for sale and distribution. While going north along the coastline, they decided to make port in one of the many secluded coves found on the Chesapeake-Virginia shore. It seemed like a good idea, but word of the cargo's arrival soon spread throughout the school-age population within one hundred miles of their landing. Within hours, kids descended upon the small community in droves. It was like a scene out of a crazy college party movie. Initially, the local troopers had no idea what was going on, but they soon figured it out. The troopers followed the traffic down to the waterfront and arrested my sailing buddies.

My friend informed me in our phone call that I would be contacted by someone the next day in my office. That Saturday before Christmas, a young man came to my office with enough financial resources for me to post bail for all six defendants and to retain the legal representation they needed to defend themselves at trial.

The story of the bust was big news. It was reported to be the largest U.S. drug bust at the time, and it attracted the attention of local prosecutors, all of whom had political careers in mind and saw the opportunity to use this event to advance their reputations. (Some of them, in fact, did go on to achieve national prominence.) Given the widespread acceptance of marijuana today, it's hard to imagine the notoriety of such events, but in those days being tough on drugs was a great way for political figures to promote their careers. The 1970s had begun with President Richard Nixon announcing his much-publicized War on Drugs campaign, and his anti-drug enforcement policies were expanded several years later under the Reagan administration.

The prosecution of drug cases was also quite different during the seventies. At the time, law enforcement officials were mostly interested in prosecuting drug crimes, not in the spoils of a crime. Why? Because in order for the government to confiscate an alleged criminal's home, boat, plane or other investments, the burden was on prosecutors to prove that these assets were obtained illegally. This was a difficult standard to meet, so unless prosecutors could readily establish other crimes resulting from these ill-gotten gains, the government would not pursue a defendant's other property. But my sailor friends' drug bust turned out to be a threshold event. After this case, the law changed. The burden of proof switched, so it became the job of the alleged drug dealer to prove that all the assets he owned were obtained legally. The net effect was that it made it possible for the government to seize virtually all property of an alleged criminal, and these assets were often never returned. Today, that law has been modified to reduce the draconian effect of this total confiscation of assets, which was proven to be unconstitutional under the search and seizure precedents set by the U.S. Supreme Court. Still, if the young sailors I befriended back then had to meet the burden of proof required of defendants today, they would not have received their bail money back when they were released from prison.

For years after this case, I got phone calls, at all times of the day and night, from individuals being prosecuted for crimes. The communication between prison inmates must be amazing! I was identified as this wizard lawyer, "Tony from New York," who could help people caught in drug busts. Early on in my career, I decided that I wasn't interested in practicing criminal law. I still wasn't. In these drug cases, my function would be limited to obtaining criminal counsel, and after doing so my involvement would end.

Nevertheless, the calls kept coming. During the course of our time on the Chesapeake, I had discussed with the young sailors my legal work smuggling the literary works of the famous Russian dissident writer, Aleksandr Solzhenitsyn, into the United States and arranging for their publication. Word must have traveled, because I started receiving unsolicited book queries from people like Lynette "Squeaky" Fromme, the infamous cult figure who attempted the assassination of President Gerald Ford.

Squeaky grew up in an ordinary middle-class household in California, the daughter of an aeronautical engineer. She never wanted for anything, but she dropped out of college in the late 1960s, got thrown out of her parents' house and. homeless, ultimately become a disciple of the murderous cult leader Charles Manson. Fromme sent me a manuscript that described how she fell prey to Manson and became absorbed into his cult. I thought the story of how she ended up joining Manson was interesting, perhaps worth publishing. But Squeaky was impossible to work with. She had no focus, and her purpose seemed mainly to be to justify her behavior and advance her own social and political agenda.

Another time, I received an incomprehensible call from serial killer Jeffrey Dahmer, in which he, too, attempted to justify his behavior. Many lesser-known criminals also contacted me to help them publish their life stories. The accounts were roughly the same—they were all innocent victims of the system. I passed.

Of the many entrepreneurs I've met over six decades, none were more resourceful and capable than those on the wrong side of the law. They impressed me as risk takers, willing to challenge conventional thought to make a lot of money—fast—and succeed in defying the system. I found a striking, if somewhat unexpected, similarity between nonviolent criminal entrepreneurs and entrepreneurs who launched legitimate businesses. Both were independent self-starters who didn't like authority and had dreams of outsmarting society. They identified a need, and then they filled it.

My sailor friends created an impressive enterprise that tackled formidable challenges. They arranged for large shipments of drugs to be delivered to them in the Bahamas at wholesale prices, and they then provided maritime transportation to elaborate distribution hubs in the United States.

Their venture demanded multiple levels of planning, and the execution of such a plan required a great deal of knowledge that any startup would need to successfully bring a product to market. I've often thought that if they, and others like them, put in as much time into legal pursuits as they did into their illegal operations, they would be very, very successful.

My young friends' story did not have a happy ending. While there were early flashes of easy wealth, they provided little opportunity for these young men to secure a normal, fulfilling life. They went through the prison system, paid their debt to society and tried to transition back to a normal life. But they never did.

Instead, they withdrew. When people spend five or six years being locked up, they often start thinking and acting in a certain way, and when they come out, they continue to think and act that way. These sailors were not innocent, but they were not evil kids. Yet as they grew older, their moral and philosophical disintegration became evident; their punishment had predestined them to a life of failure.

None of the sailors went back to school; one ended up in a mental institution. Sadly, they couldn't find ways to start over, to learn new trades, find a new circle of friends, wipe the slate clean. The process of getting things right often means going back to the point where things went wrong, and you got lost. This was something I learned from observing the experiences of others, especially young entrepreneurs. When they failed, they went back and started over. It was painful. But they discovered that when they went back and faced the obstacles that previously stopped them, they were now more adept at overcoming the same obstacles, and in doing so, they could forge a new path toward a successful future.

17

Linda Lovelace

A porn star whose ordeal lifted her into the unlikely role of feminist icon—and friend to Gloria Steinem

Many people—especially my fellow lawyers—want to know how I've come to represent clients who achieved great notoriety over the years. Beginning in the late 1960s, I had the opportunity to work on projects with several prominent artists and authors, including Russian Nobel Prize–winning novelist Aleksandr Solzhenitsyn; the popular musician and songwriter Harry Chapin; and journalists/authors such as Harrison Salisbury of *The New York Times* and *Newsday* columnists Mike McGrady and Harvey Aronson, who were good friends and shared an office in downtown Northport, near my home. Aronson had co-written *High Hopes,* a true crime book, with my law partner Jerry Sullivan, the former assistant district attorney from Suffolk County who successfully prosecuted

Ronald De Feo in the infamous "Amityville Horror" murder case.

And then there was Linda Lovelace.

"*Really?*" people would ask me. "You represented Linda Lovelace, the porn film star from *Deep Throat?* How did *that* happen?"

My relationships with high-profile figures often came about through my involvement in regional art and civic organizations, as well as referrals from other attorneys. But Linda Lovelace had an unusual back story. Her project required a series of careful and deliberate steps, like moves on a chess board, before the project could come together. And it almost didn't.

The story started with a phone call I received one day from a local attorney and friend, Victor Yannacone. Victor was a pioneer in the field of environmental law in the mid-1960s, one of the founders of the Environmental Defense Fund and an innovator in the complex and cutting-edge field of environmental litigation. He represented Kerry Ryan, whose father, Michael, was a Vietnam veteran who been exposed to Agent Orange. I had guided them in the publication of their book, *Kerry*, which spotlighted the catastrophic biological consequences suffered by children when their parents were exposed to dangerous chemicals. From lawsuits over the pesticide DDT to disputes over incinerator ash, Victor is still acknowledged as one of the most thoroughly prepared—and most abrasive—figures in environmental law. You know the slogan "Sue the bastards"? That was Victor; he coined it.

While Victor Yannacone was unquestionably a fierce litigator, he was also a true humanitarian. Victor came to me because he had taken on a client whose story he needed my help getting published. Ahh, another book. But when he told me her name, an alarm went off in my brain. I had no idea Victor had agreed to represent Linda Lovelace. Not only that, he had taken her under his wing and was treating her as if she were a family member.

It seems that Linda and her second husband, Larry Marchiano, were hiding out from her abusive ex-husband, Chuck Traynor. They were destitute, and Victor was providing them with food, money, medical care and resources to help solve their problems. This undertaking was not only Victor's; it was a cooperative effort with his wife, Carol. Linda jokingly described Victor as an unmade bed, always on the run, dragging a briefcase behind him as he raced from one place to another. She called him her Don Quixote.

By the early 1970s, Linda Lovelace had become an unwitting household name as the star of *Deep Throat,* in which she famously performed oral sex. The movie was actually the first full-length hard-core porn film; it not only made the rounds of triple-X-rated theaters but achieved wide popularity among young mainstream audiences. It even got a short review in *The New York Times* and eventually became one of the highest-grossing X-rated videotapes ever released. It's hard to fully appreciate just how shocking this was at the time; today we can easily view online porn and adult movies in the privacy of our homes.

My initial discussions with Victor were direct: I told him I had some trouble relating to his client's problems and wasn't sure I wanted to get involved. I agreed to meet with Linda before making my decision, but there were lots of questions swirling around in my mind.

First, I had to consider the reputation of my law firm. Yes, this was the 1970s—a free-wheeling era of "sex, drugs and rock 'n' roll"—but not in Huntington, Long Island. A majority of adults in our mainstream community did not look favorably upon the sexual conduct displayed in *Deep Throat.* I was a partner practicing in a traditional suburban law firm. We were a leading firm in our area, so I had to think about how a project like this would affect its identity.

There was another troubling aspect to Linda's story—the unsavory businesspeople involved with *Deep Throat*. The owner and distributor of the film was reputed to be John "Sonny" Franzese, a feared Mafia figure who was an underboss in the New York Colombo crime family. Sonny Franzese was often floated as the key person controlling the distribution of the film to movie houses all around the country. My firm had faced a similar situation when we had been asked to represent trash collectors on Long Island. This industry was allegedly associated with the mob, and there was a lot of suspicion as to whether the contracts between local municipalities and the carting companies were proper bids. Two companies had asked me to represent them as general counsel, and I turned them both down. I did not want to be associated with these people, for a firm often acquires a reputation by the people it chooses to represent.

On top of these issues, there was the basic question of whether Linda Lovelace's account was a legitimate, reliable story. Was she truly a woman trying to construct a new life, looking for a step up from a bad childhood and repeated sexual exploitation? And if so, whom could I find to write Linda's story?

I immediately thought of Mike McGrady, an icon at Long Island's leading newspaper, *Newsday*. Mike was a terrific columnist and author, with strong credentials. He studied under the novelist and poet Robert Penn Warren at Yale and was a Nieman Visiting Fellow at Harvard. He had covered both the civil rights movement and the Vietnam War, winning an Overseas Press Club Award for his columns from the front, which were later published as a book, *A Dove in Vietnam*. Mike was a serious intellectual, but he also had a wry sense of humor and an enterprising mind that would take him into uncharted literary territory.

Mike's most widely known work turned out, ironically, to be a hoax—a parody of trashy bestsellers—called *Naked Came the Stranger*, which he masterminded in the late 1960s. After plowing through Jacqueline Susann's steamy novel *Valley of the Dolls* one night, Mike decided to issue himself a challenge: to prove that any story that focused unremittingly on sex, no matter how badly written, would sell. So along with about two dozen friends at *Newsday* (all accomplished writers, including Harvey Aronson), Mike concocted a potboiler about a Long Island housewife who took revenge on her cheating husband by sleeping with as many men as possible, from a mobster to a rabbi. Each writer contributed a chapter; Mike's only instruction was that any "true excellence in writing will be quickly blue-penciled into oblivion." He kept his word.

The resulting naughty housewife novel, with Mike's sister-in-law, Penelope Ashe, as the purported author, offered absolutely no literary value. Of course, when *Naked Came the Stranger* came out in the summer of 1969, it quickly sold twenty thousand copies. And after the hoax was exposed later that summer, it gained even more notoriety, spending thirteen weeks on the *New York Times* best-seller list.

I called Mike and asked him whether he'd be interested in writing the Lovelace story. To my mild surprise, he was *very* interested. I cautioned him about the shady personalities involved in the pornography business. I described Linda's long history of exploitation and abuse. I felt that people like Linda were prone to blaming others for their behavior, deserved or not, and there was typically little understanding that somewhere along the line, they had had a chance to straighten out their lives and they hadn't. I was worried that I, Mike, our publisher and anyone else involved in this project could be added to the long list of people blamed for exploiting Linda Lovelace

But Mike was undeterred. "Tony," he said, "I have confidence in you to protect us, and I believe it's a story worth telling."

Mike also had a pretty good idea who might be interested in publishing the "real story of Linda Lovelace"—Lyle Stuart, the independent publisher known for putting out controversial titles, including *Naked Came the Stranger*. Still, I was uncomfortable. I wanted to help my friends, Victor Yannacone and Mike McGrady, but I was searching for a way to legitimize this effort, to give it more credibility and social value. Mike could see I was waffling. He said, "Let me see if Gloria Steinem would be willing to write the introduction to the book."

Mike and Gloria Steinem were social friends. A co-founder of *Ms.* magazine, Steinem had emerged as a nationally recognized leader and spokeswoman for the growing feminist movement. She had been a Playboy bunny and became a fierce women's rights advocate, fighting against female exploitation on all fronts. During this time, Mike, too, had been evolving as a feminist in his own inimitable way. During the early seventies, Mike decided to switch roles with his wife for a year, an experiment that became the basis of his book *The Kitchen Sink Papers: My Life as a Househusband.* Years later, a writer with the *Los Angeles Times* would note that Mike's experiences switching roles with his wife "turned him into a feminist, which may have influenced his decision to write two books with *Deep Throat* star Linda Lovelace."

Several days went by. Then Mike called and told me that he had lined up *both* Gloria Steinem and Lyle Stewart! Now, I was confident we could move forward with the project: We had a publisher, a reputable writer and a prominent feminist who could add credibility to the Linda Lovelace story. But I still needed to meet Linda to confirm, in my own mind, that I could represent this client properly, protecting her, as well as everyone else involved, and do something that my firm would be proud of.

Shortly thereafter, I met Linda Lovelace and her husband at my office in Huntington. They were accompanied by their not-too-friendly German shepherd, who set an unsettling tone.

Linda proceeded to relate how her former husband, Chuck Traynor, had pimped her out, abused and beat her so that she would perform the sex act that made her famous. She relayed to me how she was forcibly gang-raped, required to perform bestial and homosexual acts, sodomy, fellatio—all of which obviously humiliated her.

I had heard some of her story before. That day, she recounted the event that would appear in her book, *Ordeal,* an incident that occurred in a Florida motel room during the first day of shooting *Deep Throat.* The entire movie crew was partying in the next room, drinking, smoking pot, carrying on. Traynor called her a b—, she said, and started hitting her. "What have I done now? What was wrong?" she pleaded. "Your smile," he said. "That f— smile of yours. You were so busy smiling all day. Well, let's see how you smile now. Why don't you smile for me now?"

Linda knew the crew could hear every word. "First you yell at me because I look too sad and now you yell at me because I'm smiling too much. *Too much!* You ought to see a doctor, Chuck, you really do. Because you're crazy."

Then came the beating. "*I'm* not the one who's going to need a doctor," he said. Next door, where the crew was partying, it got as quiet as a tomb. They could hear everything. "The first punch sent me crashing onto the bed," Linda recalled. "Chuck is berserk now, picking me up off the bed and throwing me against the wall. I fall to the floor, rolling myself into a ball, protecting my stomach and breasts from his boots, screaming, 'Stop! Please stop! You're hurting me!' Screaming, 'Help! Oh, God, please help me! Someone help me!' But help does not come and the beating goes on. Why is there no help? Why do the men stay in the next room?"

As Linda told me this story, I was watching her husband for a reaction. Larry Marchiano was an intimidating fellow who seldom made eye contact but who definitely made his presence felt. He said little; he appeared to be suspicious about my advice and direction. Perhaps he *should* have been skeptical. *Deep Throat* probably had box office receipts in the tens of millions of dollars, garnering a more successful run than *Gone with the Wind*. And Linda reportedly saw no money from the film. Everybody in Linda's life had abused and exploited her. Born Linda Susan Boreman, Linda Lovelace was brought up in a working-class family in the Bronx. Her father was a New York City police officer who was seldom home; her mother a waitress who was stern and unloving. Her looks were ordinary, her personality without distinctive traits. After her father retired from the police department, the family moved to Florida. At age nineteen, Linda had a baby, which she gave up for adoption. She returned to New York to go to computer school, but she got into a car accident, sustaining serious injuries. It was while she was recovering at her parents' home that she met Chuck Traynor.

Linda didn't have a single good word to say about anybody. That day in my office, she and her husband showed little interest in the particulars concerning the publication of the book. I found myself raising my voice just to keep their attention. Linda just wanted to get the story out and be paid. After an hour, I ended the meeting and said that I would call them to review the agreement.

Two days later, Mike and I went out to lunch to discuss the book. If this project was to succeed, I told Mike, we needed to set out some very strong boundaries:

First, I would take no compensation.

Second, Mike would be paid by the publisher, not out of the proceeds that Linda received. This would further protect him from any potential claims made against him.

Third, Linda would get the best publishing agreement ever made. She would get a substantial advance, and all the monies she received would be nonrefundable. She would be insulated from any lawsuits. Once the manuscript was accepted by the publisher, the publisher would assume *all* liability related to its publication. If Linda were sued, Lyle would have to defend her at his expense and pay the judgment if she lost. And if Lyle were sued, he would have to defend the case on his own, with no rights of indemnification against Linda for financial contribution.

Mike thought these conditions seemed highly unlikely, but I believed that we needed to put up a bulletproof wall around Linda for her own protection, as well as for the protection of others involved in the project, so there could be no basis for her claiming that she was once again being exploited.

Next came the negotiation of the contract with the publisher, Lyle Stuart. It was hardly a negotiation, since I laid down our exact requirements for entering into a publishing agreement. To my amazement, Lyle accepted all the terms, without any argument.

After settling these issues, I asked Linda and her husband (their dog came, too) to meet me at my office to go over the terms of the agreement. During the meeting I had to step out of the room for a few minutes. I don't remember closing the door, but when I returned the door was closed. As I opened it, I saw Linda and Larry behind my desk, rummaging through my personal files, acting as if they were doing nothing wrong. I was not surprised. I did not confront them about their behavior. I knew they were suspicious people, to the point of paranoia, and yet extremely defensive when confronted about their own wrong conduct.

Linda Lovelace was the product of a harsh upbringing. I could understand why she might have had issues with trust and authority, why she had a natural tendency to blame others for things that happened to her. I will leave it to the psychologists to determine what influences controlled her development—whether her accusatory behavior was justified because of the treatment she received, or whether she had character flaws that facilitated (maybe even invited) her exploitation.

But I was certain that my basic reading of these folks was correct. Linda and her husband were wounded souls, and I wondered whether, if I had met them first, before my interactions with Victor Yannacone, Mike McGrady and Gloria Steinem, I would have taken them on as clients. As it turned out, the involvement of Mike and Gloria contributed enormously to my feeling that this was a worthwhile project. It convinced me that Linda's story raised some provocative issues about sex and gender in contemporary society, and this would lead us in a good direction.

Ordeal was published in 1980. In her introduction, Gloria Steinem wrote, "I want to remind all of us that to condemn pornography is not to condemn sex, not even to condone censorship. The question is free will: Are the subjects of pornography there by choice, or by coercion, economic or physical?" She implored readers to make the distinction between pornography and erotica, between domination and mutual choice. She made good arguments; I hoped people would see the difference.

The advance, royalties and added compensation gave Linda Lovelace enough financial support to provide a transition into a more normal life. She tried to launch a career as an actress, but her reputation barred her from any substantial success, either on stage or in subsequent films. Interestingly, Linda and Gloria Steinem became close friends. Linda became an anti-pornography activist, speaking before feminist groups and at colleges, even testifying before the Attorney General's Commission on Pornography in 1986.

Linda Lovelace and Larry Marchiano settled down on Eastern Long Island and had two children together. For a while, her life seemed stable, but she continued to fight health issues for years because of the silicone injected into her breasts that had migrated to her kidneys and liver. When Marchiano's drywall business went bankrupt, they moved to Colorado. She divorced him several years later and died at fifty-three from injuries suffered in another automobile accident.

In the end, our team was able to fulfill all the goals of the project, bringing the story to publication without raising any objections from Linda. She was not sued; she got all the money she was promised. Mike McGrady would write another book with Linda, *Out of Bondage,* and he later became a film and restaurant critic for *Newsday.* My law firm? Well, I suppose the old saying, "There's no such thing as bad publicity," is often true. In combination with our representation of people like Aleksandr Solzhenitsyn and Harry Chapin, Linda's case blended in a way that generated a fair amount of interest in our firm's diverse capabilities and clientele.

And whatever you think of Linda Lovelace as a person, there was no question she had a significant story to tell. I believe it changed people's views of women and their sexuality. It held a mirror up to society that said that the way we were making judgments about the sexual conduct of women and not about the men involved with them reflected our prejudices against women. That hypocrisy was palpable, and it continues today, as we can see from the ongoing saga of Monica Lewinsky.

Learning about the exploitation of women was also an important educational process for me. During my life I was largely influenced by four powerful women around me: my mother; my best friend's mother, Anne De Noto; my wife, Linda; and my law partner, Barbara Alesi. I certainly respected these women, but I saw them as being able to control their circumstances, never in need of protection. Over time, however, I became aware that there are many women not as able to protect themselves. Seeing Linda Lovelace through the lens of Gloria Steinem and Mike McGrady, I got much needed lessons in the women's movement and the issues of sexual exploitation, for which I will always be grateful.

So ultimately, when I think back to the question people asked me, "How did you come to represent celebrities like Linda Lovelace?" I believe that I simply followed this maxim: Do good work. What this meant for me, whether working with Solzhenitsyn or with Linda Lovelace, was to stay assiduously on my toes, to ensure that every action was disclosed every step of the way. I wanted to make sure that if I looked back in time, a year or two from now, I could demonstrate the appropriateness of the conduct and actions of all the players—including me.

That was always a good test. It was something I first learned practicing securities and exchange law: You need to disclose to your investors all the pertinent facts in a case, because if you don't, and one of these facts becomes the subject of a lawsuit, you'll find yourself looking back and saying, "My God, why didn't we disclose that fact?" It was important to communicate fully, always disclosing all the facts, warning your client of the difficulties and risks that could occur in any case.

Lawyers are sometimes reluctant to communicate such things. They may be worried that clients feel their lawyer is not sufficiently advocating in their interests; that they will be criticized, even sued. But especially with people who have a track record of feeling victimized, proper representation means making sure that the actions meet the standards of appropriate conduct. You need to disclose the facts, identify the risks and take it from there. Forewarned is forearmed— for both you *and* your client.

Whether they're literary celebrities or construction workers, your clients will tell their friends if you represented them fairly and properly, and you will inevitably create a following. And if a case is referred to you by another lawyer, so much the better. What I've learned in relationships with attorneys like Victor Yannacone is that lawyers who refer cases to you often become a source that generates a steady stream of similar cases. For that reason, they deserve special attention—and they, in turn, will give special attention to attorneys they trust.

18

Martyn and Margaret Clark

*A magical seafaring couple from Nova Scotia who
revealed what had been my life's mission*

I t was in the fall of 1969, shortly after the United States
landed a man on the moon, when a small, weather-beaten
ship sailed into Long Island's Northport Harbor and
anchored.

It looked like the *Bluenose*, the famous schooner designed
in 1921 for racing but widely known as queen of the North
Atlantic fleet that fished the Grand Banks off the Canadian coast for decades. The *Bluenose* became the pride of
Nova Scotia (the name was originally a nickname for Nova
Scotians), and in 1937 the Canadian dime was changed to
include an image of the iconic ship. This boat, however, was
much shorter. Its length was closer to thirty-five feet while
the length of the *Bluenose* was one hundred feet.

I was taking an evening sail in my nineteen-foot dinghy
when I first noticed the vessel. I was intrigued by the Cana-

dian flag flying from its stern. Having spent some time on the water, I knew that if a boat had its hatch and portholes open, it was likely that somebody was on board, and if I sailed around it a few times someone would likely come on deck.

Sure enough, a young man appeared. I decided to strike up a conversation with him. He was serious but friendly, and I learned that he had sailed from Nova Scotia with his bride on their honeymoon voyage, which would take them to Vancouver, British Columbia, in the year ahead. They both had graduated from the University of Toronto, he with a degree in English literature, she with a degree in nursing. What an interesting couple!

That was how I met Martyn and Margaret Clark. Martyn and Margaret were a matched set that looked as if they had come from the same family, with one difference: When Martyn spoke, he had a tendency to move away, while Margaret would move closer in her conversations.

Over the next three weeks we spent a good deal of time together. I became absorbed in their adventure: Martyn's plan was to sail their schooner, *Ayesha,* down the eastern shore of the Americas to the West Indies after the hurricane season had ended and before the winter storms started. I tried to get him to stay the winter so I could find him a job and he could finish the more important work that needed to be done on the boat to make it shipshape for the rugged sea trials ahead. But he was adamant about leaving. Martyn had a plan. And he wanted to keep on schedule.

Resigned to their departure, I showed the couple around town, introducing them to the local marinas where they could obtain some ship stores and essential marine products. We had numerous conversations during which I would take the measure of this man and his wife. They were intelligent and industrious and had wonderful plans for their future, filled with unconventional and adventurous undertakings. They had no guarantees for work and little money, but they had a plan for what they wanted to do and where they wanted to go. Theirs was totally unlike my predictable life: high school, college, law school, marriage, job, mortgage and children. The Clarks were not captured by any ideals of conformity.

The day soon came when they would have to set sail. The night before their departure I threw them a small dinner party at the local bistro. We had gathered some ship stores to help them along the way and discreetly passed them some cash to keep the sharks away from their stern.

I wasn't sure why I was so open to meeting the Clarks and lending them a helping hand, but their love of the sea and its challenges created an unexpected level of excitement in me; somehow, I wanted to help them realize their dreams. Maybe it was because I dreamed of doing the same thing. Or maybe it was because I was reading Joshua Slocum's chronicle about his solo trip circumnavigating the globe on the thirty-six-foot wooden schooner *Spray*. Born in Nova Scotia, Slocum was a rough-edged nineteenth-century captain who set sail from Boston on a three-year, 46,000-mile voyage. Slocum's autobiographical account is filled with wonderful stories; anyone with a love for the sea would be mesmerized by it. Coincidentally, the Clarks had left Nova Scotia from a place very near where Slocum was born, so maybe that was also a connection.

The afternoon before they left, I went to a local jewelry store and found a pair of Canadian dime *Bluenose* schooner earrings that had been cast in silhouette. That evening I presented the earrings to Margaret, and our box of stores to Martyn. And when Martyn and Margaret set sail the next morning, I felt as if I had lost some dear friends.

Fast-forward 30 years.

When I got home from work one day in the late summer of 1998, my wife told me that Captain Clark had tried to dock at the Northport town wharf, but because the water wasn't deep enough, he had to find suitable moorings at Danford's marina restaurant in Port Jefferson, twenty miles east of Northport. Not once in thirty years had I heard from the Clarks, although they had crossed my mind from time to time. They said they would tie up for the night at Danford's and hoped I would meet them for a reunion, albeit a short one. Without a second thought, I rearranged my schedule so I could be with them for the evening.

Before heading east, I called Freeman McNeil, a former all-pro running back for the New York Jets who had been my client in a historic antitrust suit against the National Football League. Several years earlier, on my fiftieth birthday, Freeman had given me a pair of *Bluenose* schooner cufflinks, cut just like the earrings I had given Margaret in 1968. Freeman and I were close friends, and I thought it serendipitous that he had selected this gift for me on my birthday. I told him the story of meeting the Clarks and my gift to Margaret years ago. When I asked him for permission to regift the cufflinks to Martyn, he enthusiastically agreed. So when I arrived at dockside, I was doubly excited: first, to see the Clarks after all these years; and second, to pair Margaret's *Bluenose* earrings with Martyn's new cufflinks.

Their new schooner was impressive. It was more than double the size of their old boat, manned by a crew of tanned, athletic-looking youngsters. Martyn and Margaret had founded a premier offshore sailing school called the Sail and Life Training Society (S.A.L.T.S.), whose mission was to teach young people life lessons that can only be learned by going to sea. Over the years, the couple had logged hundreds of thousands of nautical miles with their S.A.L.T.S. trainees, growing the society's school and summer and offshore programs while taking on occasional restoration and consulting projects.

After the usual hellos this summer evening, things settled down and I suddenly noticed that Margaret wearing the *Bluenose* schooner earrings I had given her thirty years earlier. It was then that I presented the *Bluenose* cufflinks to Martyn.

What a wonderful reunion! We caught up and shared some stories, and it got late quickly. They were leaving the next morning, so again, I had to say goodbye to dear friends. This time, our parting was made easier by the fact that I knew that they were achieving their life's dreams. Much of what we had spoken of years earlier they were accomplishing, and in a way that brought credit to themselves as well as paying homage to marine history. They were restoring old schooners and continuing to sail to far-flung destinations, teaching the next generation the ways of the sea. You just can't quantify the benefits they were bestowing on the young people whose lives would be forever changed by their experiences circumnavigating the world.

Fast-forward another 20 years.

Over the next several years, I had kept loose track of the Clarks but had had no direct contact. Then, in November 2018, I received an email from one of the Clarks' daughters (they had five) inviting me to help celebrate their parents' fiftieth wedding anniversary in July 2019. It would take place in Broad Cove, Nova Scotia. At the time, I was having back problems and was unable to walk long distances without pain. I had been struggling with the decision to have spinal surgery or not, and it became clear that if I wanted to go to the celebration, I had better make up my mind. I just knew I had to make the trip from New York.

I took out the calendar, looked at the amount of time between the end of November and the end of July, the time of the celebration. I thought there might be enough time, so I immediately contacted the surgeons and laid out a schedule for my surgery and convalescence. The date of the surgery was set, and the rehab period was long enough to give me a little extra time, if needed. After rehab I finally got the green light, and with the help of and my surgeon and my secretary, Adrienne, I was set to go to Nova Scotia.

I couldn't wait to find out how the final chapter of the Clarks' life was playing out. I had been in touch with the daughters, who relayed the story their parents had told them about landing in Northport harbor fifty years earlier. The story was not only alive in my mind; it was alive in theirs.

When I arrived in Nova Scotia on July 26, a small private dinner at the Clarks' modest home was arranged. I was greeted with a friendliness and warmth that made me certain I had made the right decision in coming. The first night was an intimate reunion, a buffet dinner with family and some close friends. The next day was the main anniversary celebration, held in a small, rustic meeting house. It was clear that the family was among loving and thoughtful people, all of whom knew that the Clarks were special. We began with a grace that was sung before dinner. It was their usual custom, what they did every day, but what a blessing it was—rousing, enthusiastic singing enjoyed by all!

I was asked to say a few words for the occasion, and I thought I should explain why this couple had attracted me so much that—five decades later—I needed to be part of their fiftieth wedding celebration.

I had been thinking about this a few months earlier, still trying to understand my fascination with the Clarks. Then, as I began writing this book, I hit on a profound personal insight: I realized that my life's goal was imbedded in helping people who had bold ideas; I saw those people as the heroes of our time. When I first met Martyn and Margaret

I didn't know this was my life's path. But as I looked back, I saw that this scenario has played out exactly that way, one story or case at a time, repeated over and over during my professional life. When I met people with dreams, energy, intelligence and character who had a quest, I was immediately drawn to them—and I wanted to help.

I explained all this to the anniversary gathering, how I was drawn to the Clarks' adventurous quest as part of my own unfolding mission. It didn't surprise me that I was surrounded by people who shared my admiration for this outstanding couple. They knew the Clarks were a cut above, living out their dream of service and charity.

Since the anniversary celebration in Nova Scotia I have exchanged numerous emails and letters with the Clarks, and I continue to be amazed by them and their adventures. I regret that over the prior fifty years I did not remain close enough to enjoy in "real time" their stories as they unfolded. But I have since corrected that!

I'm not sure exactly when I will see Martyn and Margaret Clark again, but it doesn't matter. I've seen what life can be like when all the pieces fit. I know that the rest of their lives will be filled with new adventures and great memories that are equal to their evolving aspirations. And to have had a small, precious part in their adventures…well, that is reward enough for me.

19

Martin Luther King

*The singular celebration that memorialized America's
quest for racial justice and equality*

In the summer of 1985, I was invited to a meeting hosted by Jack English, the managing partner of my law firm at the time, Suozzi English & Klein. I wasn't told the purpose of the meeting, but I knew it was something important. From the list of invitees, I could see that Jack had assembled an imposing group of power brokers.

Among them was my friend Basil Patterson, a partner at Suozzi English, former State Senator from Harlem and past Secretary of State for New York under Governor Hugh Carey. Basil was the father of David Paterson, who roughly twenty years later would become Lieutenant Governor of New York and then Governor, after a scandal forced the resignation of Elliot Spitzer. Also in attendance was Harold Ickes, who would be named White House Deputy Chief of Staff for President Bill Clinton, and Lloyd Williams, President of the Uptown Chamber of Commerce for the City of New York, an impressive man whom I met for the first time. Jack English, himself, was a highly influential leader in national, state and local Democratic politics. He served as a top advisor to the Kennedys and would later play a key role in the election of several U.S. Senators and other prominent politicians.

After the usual pleasantries, we got down to business. Almost two years earlier, on November 2, 1983, President Ronald Reagan had signed into law a bill that established a federal holiday honoring Martin Luther King Jr. The first observance of the holiday would be January 20th, 1986, and coinciding with this date, the task before our group was to establish the MLK Living the Dream Foundation and present a live prime-time program, consisting of a two-hour ABC TV network television special broadcast from three separate forums: Hollywood, Atlanta and New York City. Jack pronounced that this inaugural celebration was to be inspirational and entertaining, but that was extent of the planning. Nothing else had been decided. Then Jack turned to me. "We would like *you* to give structure to the evening," he said. "What do you mean, 'give structure to the evening?'" I asked. As he explained the scope of the project, I began to see the enormity of the undertaking.

At the outset, a New York charitable foundation had to be created. The entity would be income tax-free, with state and U.S. tax-exemption to provide a deduction for donors to the event. Contracts between the foundation and ABC Network had to be negotiated for the production of a TV special, with the proceeds allocated among the three venues to cover their respective costs. Accountants had to be hired and committees formed to administer the many services essential to make this big night memorable and financially successful.

My first thought was that this was a job for a first-rate theatrical promoter. Not me! But after some arm-twisting, my colleagues convinced me that I was the right choice, since I had a fair amount of experience structuring comprehensive plans that required a lot of moving parts. Besides, this was a great opportunity for the law firm to present its capabilities before a national audience, as well as participate in an important national event.

There was no question, of course, that this celebration would mark a pivotal moment in U.S. history. Martin Luther King Jr. was a Baptist minister and President of Southern Christian Leadership Conference, who aspired to be a leading voice for civil rights in the South. He ended up becoming much more—a major moral force for the entire nation. Before being assassinated in 1968 at age 39, King had already been awarded the Nobel Peace Prize and led a non-violent movement of millions of blacks and whites that forever impacted racial segregation in this country. His passionate advocacy for civil and human rights, rooted in the strategies of peaceful demonstration adopted by Mahatma Gandhi, brought a new dimension of dignity to people's lives and renewed hope for freedom in the community of man. His soaring oratory and powerful presence, coupled with the strength of his vision, not only impassioned people of this country, but countries around the world.

Even so, the road to MLK Day had not been an easy one. The fight for this holiday had been an epic struggle in and of itself. The first push to establish a federal holiday honoring King came from John Conyers, a Democratic Representative from Michigan, who presented a bill to Congress calling for the holiday just four days after King's assassination. It failed. And when he introduced the same bill year after year, it failed again and again, while gathering co-sponsors along the way. The tide turned in the 1980s, with the help of persistent advocates like the Coretta Scott King, Martin's widow, and the Congressional Black Caucus, which had collected six million signatures for a petition in support of a holiday for King. Stevie Wonder had written a popular song, "Happy Birthday," about King, which bolstered the campaign. Finally, despite filibusters in the Senate, Congress passed legislation creating the federal holiday honoring King, and President Reagan signed it into law.

Now that the law was going into effect in six months, it was up to our committee to usher in the celebration. So I accepted my weighty assignment, but upon leaving the meeting I turned to my law partner, Barbara Alesi, for help and guidance. She and I had worked together on a number of projects with great success, and I trusted her legal skills and judgment. Once more, they would come in handy.

Our first task was to help organize a cocktail party for the proposed event committee members and donors. The party was held at the duplex apartment of Andrew Stein in the Upper East Side in Manhattan. Stein was a former Manhattan Borough President; his father, Jerry Finkelstein, was the multi-millionaire owner and publisher of the New York Law Journal and was a major influence in the business and legal affairs of the city. The party was packed with notables, including Coretta Scott King, Mayor Edward Koch, Manhattan Borough President David Dinkins, former Borough President Percy Sutton, and future U.S. President, Donald J. Trump. Andrew Stein had preceded Percy Sutton as Manhattan Borough President and he was succeeded by David Denkins, who then succeeded Koch as mayor. All the power brokers were aligned!

At one point, when pledges were being made, I was standing between Koch and Trump, both of whom were avid supporters of the holiday. Overall, the enthusiasm for the occasion was palpable, and having worked on several charitable events, I felt that our fundraising goals were going to be an easy reach.

They were fifty co-chairmen and forty associate chairmen lined up to serve, although I had no idea what they would do. We also had patrons and a working committee, numbering forty more people. When it came time to set a date for our first planning meeting, it wasn't clear how many of these 130 participants would actually attend; nevertheless, had to provide for a facility that was large enough if they all came. I would have preferred our law office conference room in Mineola, Long Island, but I was concerned it might be too small. We were told that the Adam Clayton Powell building in Harlem, named after the famed congressman, would be a suitable place for our meetings. So the first meeting was scheduled, announcements were made, and invitations sent out.

We shouldn't have worried about the room. At our first working session, only twelve people showed up—including Barbara Alesi and me. With the group on hand, we established sub-committees for ticket sales, community involvement, promotion and advertising, entertainment and fundraising. We broke down each targeted community we needed to reach in order to sell out Radio City Music Hall, the legendary Manhattan venue that held 4,000-plus people. In particular, we had 500 seats in the orchestra that needed to be sold for $500 each, and these seats represented a substantial portion of the monies that we were hoping to raise from the live event. Every task was identified, and people were put in charge of each of them. Since many internationally known artists were scheduled to perform, we had to provide for their accommodations and hospitality. By the end of the meeting two hours later, we felt comfortable that we understood what was needed to have a successful celebration, and I scheduled a date for the next meeting.

When we met two weeks later, thinking that we had made some important progress, we were shocked to find out how little was actually done. It was a classic example of the challenge facing major volunteer initiatives. In business, autocracy is the standard. People are assigned jobs and told what to do and people do it. In organizations supported by volunteers, leadership is not autocratic; it is cooperative. Most workers are volunteers, so each person must be coaxed to perform their respective jobs and given the support they need to carry them out. The adjustment in leadership needed to navigate between these two universes is demanding, and it's often the difference between succeeding and failing in the job.

While there was lots of discussion, with lots of good ideas about how to accomplish things, our committee members had to be pushed to complete the assignments. For weeks, Barbara and I would take turns urging them to deliver what they had agreed to do. Ultimately, everyone carried out their responsibilities, but it was touch-and-go, right up to the night of the event.

With fundraisers being carried out in three cities, our collective target for this event was a half million dollars, to be donated to the King Center in Atlanta. As a charitable entity, the foundation would be under scrutiny by both the New York State Attorney General's office and the Internal Revenue Service, so we had to be mindful of our obligations to keep accurate and complete records to support our government filings. We set up finance committee to oversee this task, and were confident that they could do the job, as long as they were given the needed support.

Unfortunately, this record-keeping was never done to my satisfaction. There were too many people authorized to collect and disburse monies, making it almost impossible to set up the procedures necessary for accurate reporting. In the end, we had to piece together a number of donations and expenses to complete the official record of the event. Once again, this was not unusual for volunteer-driven charitable activities. The intentions of volunteers were not always matched by their deeds.

Nevertheless, the night of the event was spectacular. Radio City Music Hall was packed with a revved-up crowd, ready for a night of celebration, outstanding theatrical performances, and the joy of honoring the accomplishments of a great man. I was ushered backstage into the labyrinth of staging areas, rehearsal facilities and dressing rooms—the operational guts of Radio City Music Hall. I had been to Radio City Music Hall many times, starting at the age of 10, but I'd never been on the other side of the curtain. And while I was not new to being in front of crowds, nothing prepared me for what I confronted backstage. There were literally dozens of people sporadically moving around, each with a different task, all seemingly unrelated. With only minutes before showtime, the scene appeared utterly chaotic. How could they bring this mess together to create a memorable night?

Yet when the time came, the entire crew moved with the precision of a fine watch. As the show was set to open, I would be in position to welcome the volunteers, donors and audience, and thank them all for their participation. Then, when the cue was given, I would kick off the festivities. And that's just what happened. As the curtain rose, I stepped forward, and the evening unfolded into a wonderfully smooth presentation of star-studded entertainment.

At the time, Whitney Houston was a relative newcomer, but her presence and performance stunned the audience. What a voice, what a performance! She was joined by her cousin, Dionne Warwick, comedian Bill Cosby, and singers Neil Diamond, Harry Belafonte, Bette Midler and Lionel

Richie. One performance after another, each framed by a message recalling the historic achievements of Martin Luther King's life. It was an inspiring event, whether you saw it on television or in person.

The raves came from all quarters, and we were gratified by the night's success. In commercial terms, some might have considered it an "easy sale." A national holiday, celebrating a great man. What could have gone wrong? Well, a lot, but thankfully, it all worked out. Several nights later, Governor Mario Cuomo presented me with the MLK Living the Dream Foundation Medal at the Harlem Community Center, an award I cherish to this day.

Once the dust had settled, the job of "cleanup" began. First, we had to make the rounds to secure all the monetary pledges made to the King Center. While most people honored their pledges, some large would-be donors coincidentally became "very difficult to reach." Eventually, we had to abandon our efforts to collect their pledges; we simply left them to harbor their own memories of dishonor.

After we had collected several outstanding pledges over the next year, the plan was for Lloyd Williams, the Uptown Chamber of Commerce President, to join me in a trip from New York to California to meet with Stevie Wonder's business group, Black Bull Productions. Lloyd was the driving force behind the night's success and continued to support the project every step of the way. After securing the donation from Black Bull, we would travel to Atlanta to present all the pledges to Mrs. King.

The office of Black Bull Productions was located in a commercial building in downtown Los Angeles. There were glass partitions between its waiting room and the electronic message board of the New York Stock Exchange, and while we were sitting there it was natural for me to watch the trading taking place. Little did I know it would be a consequential day in stock market history. It was called Black Monday. In a matter of hours, the Dow Jones Industrial Average lost more than 500 points. The loss represented a 22 percent drop in the Dow and almost a 50 percent decline in the total value of all companies in the U.S. TV commentators said that the market fell faster than skydiver without a parachute. The events of that day were being compared to the Great Depression, with warnings of similar events. What a day to ask for money!

I was spellbound by the scene, and as I was ruminating about this loss of wealth, Lloyd made a comment I'll never forget: "In the black community we get used to these kinds of events," he said. "It happens every day." Finally, after a wait of several hours in which I soaked up the calamity of the stock market, Stevie Wonder's agent appeared from behind closed doors and presented us with a check.

When we first left New York for LA, we had hoped to make the trip in one day but the delay in collecting Stevie Wonder's pledge had turned the trip into a two-day excursion. During the long bicoastal flights, Lloyd and I had extensive conversations about the successes and failures of our kick-off event at Radio City Music Hall. We concluded that the failures were small, and the major achievements were real; only an edgy critic would nitpick its shortcomings. The funds raised for the King Center were less than half what we had hoped, but they were still a meaningful contribution.

On the following morning, as we were preparing for the last leg of the trip, Lloyd and I had chance to chat over breakfast. He told me the trip to Atlanta had two purposes: one was to deliver the pledges; the other was to deliver *me*, so Mrs. King could discuss my future involvement with the Center. The King Center, he said, was looking for board members and my work had come to her attention. Lloyd thought she might ask me to serve on the board. I was bit surprised, but not shocked. I had worked hard for the foundation and had a lot of influential people tooting my horn. I was intrigued by the opportunity to work closely in support of the legacy of an amazing man who changed the course of America. We caught an early flight from LA to Atlanta and I thought long and hard about it during the trip. When we arrived, I decided that if offered, I would accept a position on the board.

We took a cab to the King Center and when we arrived we were brought into a small conference room. Shortly thereafter, we were greeted by Mrs. King, who was accompanied by a man introduced to us as the executive director of the center. I had met Mrs. King once before at the opening cocktail party at Andrew Stein's apartment, but I did not have a chance to speak with her then. I was looking forward to this one-on-one discourse and the opportunity to personally present the pledges of support for the center—the culmination of six month's effort by the foundation.

After the thank you's and expressions of mutual appreciation, I inquired about the work of the center, which was founded by Mrs. King. Within the black community Mrs. King was regarded as the "black Madonna." Although she was best known as the wife of Martin, working side-by-side with her husband, Coretta Scott King had established a distinguished career as civil rights activist in her own right. She was friends with many prominent politicians, including the Kennedy family and President Lyndon B. Johnson, and she worked to pass the 1964 Civil Rights Act. Coretta was also a talented singer, who incorporated her passion for music into political activism.

Mrs. King recounted the story of Rosa Parks, a 42-year-old seamstress who was arrested in 1955 as for refusing to give up her seat on a bus to a white man. This event caused a spontaneous demonstration and sparked a reaction among the black community that mobilized more than 42 leaders to organize the Montgomery Improvement Association, and they elected Dr. King president. The new organization responded swiftly, initiating the Montgomery Bus Boycott, a movement that catapulted Dr. King to national prominence as a leader in the struggle for civil rights.

She went on to explain the work of the center, which had been collaborating with the U.S. Armed Forces, interacting directly with military chaplains on interracial, interpersonal and human relations programs to promote the resolution of conflicts nonviolently. Through its components of scholarship and internship programs, the center assisted graduate and undergraduate students in the development of leadership skills for non-violent social change. Academic seminars on philosophy and strategy were organized and information of their findings were disseminated.

I asked Mrs. King about how the Center's progress was being measured. She responded that she was satisfied with the progress being made, acknowledging that much more had to be done, but she thought they were on the right track. I then presented her the checks, explaining that we were sorry that it was not more. She said she understood.

Mrs. King then shifted the conversation to the future work of the center. As she began to speak, she interrupted herself, taking her shoes off and placing her feet on a chair next to me, complaining that her feet were "barking." I felt very much at home, free to speak my mind. She told me that before an offer was made to any board candidate, she wanted to discuss their vision of what their contribution to the Center might be.

I hadn't much time to prepare for this interview, but I said I thought the country was ready to make a major push, putting a spotlight on racial discrimination. I believed that money and political support for this movement would be forthcoming from the white community, and I wanted to maximize the impact of this cultural sea change, matching the country's commitment to racial justice with demonstrable performance of the black community. I emphasized that the burden for black America going forward would not be easy. It had to be accomplished in spite of all the difficulties and obstacles, starting with the issues of family relations, community, scholarship and ending in achievement—and accountability. Mrs. King and the Executive Director listened intently. She agreed that we were standing at a critical moment, when the advancement of the black community could be a shining example of all that Dr. King stood for. It was enormous responsibility for the black community to accept the challenge of meeting these goals—and go beyond it.

I left the meeting hoping that my message was understood, but I wasn't sure. I believed there was great commonality in our respective goals, yet I sensed that I had not fully communicated my thoughts. I recognize, too, that my manner can be strong at times and perhaps it was misunderstood. In time, I received confirmation that I was no longer under consideration for becoming a trustee at the King Center.

Nevertheless, I believe today what I believed then. Work has to be done on both sides, black and white, to achieve the goals of Martin Luther King Jr. All right-thinking Americans must join in spirit at the highest level so that both black and white communities can reach the lofty goals promised by our forefathers. Effort with accountability. That's what it will take to unite us, to bond us as one family with mutual respect for achievement, fairly recognized by *both* communities.

That was the message I wanted to convey to Mrs. King that day in Atlanta. Whether I did or not, I know this was the goal of Dr. King. And I was proud to have played a part in inaugurating the national holiday in honor of Martin Luther King. Through all his struggles, challenges, setbacks and successes, he was truly one of select group of extraordinary Americans who changed the course of history through persistence of their own unique vision, a mind of their own.

ACKNOWLEDGMENTS

No one does anything fully alone. We all benefit from the gifts and influences of others.

Thank you, Linda, for your love, devotion and support during the writing of this book and for its title, *A Mind of Their Own*.

I so appreciate the hard work and support of Ron Roel, who has edited these chapters. Without his efforts, these stories would not have shined as brightly.

A special thanks to my team at Onward Publishing, who made the book a reality, especially publisher Jeff Barasch.

I also would like to thank my friends and colleagues who read early versions of the manuscript and offered valuable feedback and words of encouragement as I entered unknown territory.

Lastly, my heartfelt thanks to all the entrepreneurs and law partners I have worked with over these many years. You have inspired me. You have motivated me. You have enriched my life. And, while there are far too many to recognize individually in this book, please know the depth of my gratitude. Each of you—your ideas, aspirations and achievements—has made my life as a lawyer ever more meaningful.